GREAT SOCCER STARS

To, JOHN
from, CAROLE
HAPPY Birthday

Hamlyn London · New York · Sydney · Toronto

JIMMY HILL
GREAT SOCCER STARS

**The pictures on the endpapers and in the
preliminary pages are as follows:**
endpapers
**Alan Ball, perpetual motion in a football
shirt, in this case Arsenal's.**
half-title
Uwe Seeler of West Germany in acrobatic pose.
title-page
**A superb jump by Geoff Hurst to get in a header
while surrounded by defenders.**
facing introduction
**Emlyn Hughes with the European Cup, won by
Liverpool in 1977 and 1978.**

Published by
The Hamlyn Publishing Group Limited
London · New York · Sydney · Toronto
Astronaut House, Feltham, Middlesex, England

Copyright © Jimmy Hill 1978

ISBN 0 600 38334 2

Filmset in England by
Tradespools Limited, Frome, Somerset
Printed in England by
Hazell Watson & Viney Ltd, Aylesbury, Bucks

Contents

The 100 great soccer stars analysed by Jimmy Hill are
listed below. The players appear in alphabetical order
throughout the book.

Introduction

One hundred great footballers. It was quite a job
choosing them. When I consider the number of fine
players I have left out I am glad we did not decide to call
the book the hundred greatest footballers. For that would
have been impossible – and unfair.

So what have I looked for in this compilation?
I have tried to select players who have impressed me
with some particular talent or some particular personality.
And when I have gone back through the years, I have
tried to name the players who were doing something
special in their time. I came into football early enough to
talk many hours away with those who saw the greats of the
past and I do not have to justify my choice to myself.

The reader may think differently, and to him I can
only suggest that he tries to name a hundred. I am certain
we would differ in many respects.

But I am also certain that the exercise would give him
as many hours of pleasure as compiling this book has given
me. Walking down the paths of yesteryear has been
stimulating. I sincerely hope that this book has the same
effect on the reader.

Great Soccer Stars

Ivor Allchurch

Wales, Swansea Town, Newcastle United, Cardiff City, Swansea Town

An inside-forward of the traditional school, Allchurch had complete control over the ball. He was a lovely, fluent mover, so fluent that he did not change gears, he was always in automatic drive.

He was a goalscorer, too, at a rate beyond most of today's strikers. But best of all, he was the boss in his opponents' half. Long passes or short passes, they were no trouble to Ivor, and he had a body swerve that wingers envied.

On top of all that, he had elegance. The game never seemed to be going too fast for him.

The golden boy of Welsh football of the 1950s, Ivor Allchurch.

Perhaps he was not the greatest defender in the true sense of the phrase, which demands that midfield players spend some time in their own half. But how many wing-halves who were supposed to be looking after him found time for attacking duties?

Wales will find few more loyal servants than Ivor. His League career began with nine seasons at Swansea Town and ended with another three. The only time he strayed across the border was for a four-year spell at Newcastle when he had finally, and sadly, convinced himself that his ambitions could never be realised at Swansea.

Allchurch made his Swansea debut in the 1949-50 season and won his first cap for Wales the following year. For the next 15 years, the Welsh policy was to put Allchurch's name down first, then pick the other ten.

These were exciting times at Swansea. They felt they had the team to reach the First Division, and it is true that by 1955 they had only one uncapped player in the side. Promotion always seemed probable, but never became a reality. The dream was shattered forever when the fat cheque books of affluent English teams enticed most of Swansea's stars.

John Charles went to Leeds, Mel Charles to Arsenal, Terry Medwin and Cliff Jones to Tottenham. Allchurch, temporarily at least, refused to give way.

The 1958 World Cup almost became a personal triumph for Allchurch when his goals against Mexico and Hungary swept the Welsh into the quarter-finals. There, they lost to Brazil – but only just.

Perhaps that tournament increased his appetite for the big time. Whatever the truth, he finally sacrificed his ideal and agreed to join Newcastle for £20,000.

In Geordieland, he shared the inside-forward positions with George Eastham, England's wispy creator. He scored 16 times in 26 games during his first season there and all seemed to be well. But, as he admitted later, Newcastle was not a happy club. By 1962, Ivor was back in his beloved homeland, this time on the books of Cardiff City.

It was during 1962 that Allchurch won his 49th cap for Wales, beating Billy Meredith's record. He was to go on, however, and his 68 caps is still a record today.

Ivor's international swansong was spectacular. In late 1965, he came close to destroying the England defence which was to secure the World Cup within a year. That match, at Ninian Park, finished goalless, but even the normally reserved Sir Alf Ramsey was moved to comment afterwards: 'Allchurch was a great player out there today.'

Back at Swansea, Ivor played more than a century of League games in his final three seasons, before waving an emotional farewell on a May night in 1968.

Leeds United provided the opposition for Ivor's testimonial, and he went out the way that every Welshman would like to remember him.

Although he later went on to play for Worcester City and Haverfordwest in non-league football, to me and thousands of others he will always remain Ivor Allchurch, Swansea Town and Wales.

Pietro Anastasi

Italy, Cantania, Varese, Juventus

Sicily is not noted for footballers of rare quality, but in Pietro Anastasi this beautiful Mediterranean island had one of the world's most brilliant players.

He hailed from Catania, for whom he set out on a career of spectacular success. While still in his 'teens he joined Varese in the Italian First Division, who seemed more alert to his unfinished skills than most of the better known clubs—and what a profitable

piece of judgement it proved. Two years later the Turin club, Juventus, under the affluent aegis of Umberto Agnelli, the millionaire head of the Fiat motor company, paid £440,000 for Anastasi's services, of which the player was reputed to have pocketed £23,500 as his share of the transaction.

By that time he had already played for Italy at Under-23 level and was seen in England in December, 1966, but like his compatriots he was confounded by a frozen pitch in Nottingham, Martin Chivers giving England a narrow 1-0 success.

Characteristically, once he had joined Juventus Anastasi was quickly launched into the full Italian side and some observers from afar felt the introduction had come too soon.

Not Anastasi. He thrived on being tossed into the 1968 European Championship Final against Yugoslavia after the first match had been drawn 1-1, and he scored the decisive second goal which, with Riva's, brought this

Pietro Anastasi, a Sicilian, who made his mark with Juventus and Italy.

much-sought prize to Italy for the first time.

Juventus grew in power and in 1972 and 1973 they won the domestic championship. Throughout the build-up years to those successes and subsequently, Anastasi was both creating and scoring many excellent goals.

I used to enjoy the completeness of the man. He was quick, strong and extremely difficult to check once in stride. When the ball was crossed to him in attacking situations he could time his jump to such perfection that often goalkeepers had barely reacted by the time the ball was flashing past them.

He caused English players a few problems, notably at the Communale Stadium in Turin one June night in 1973 – a night, in fact, when Italy beat England for the first time in nine meetings going back 40 years.

The game was almost 40 minutes old when Anastasi pounced on a parried shot in the goalmouth and thumped the rebound between Bobby Moore's legs into the net. In the second half it was his long sweeping pass to the wing which set up a second goal for the Italians, this time finished off by Capello.

Alan Ball

England, Blackpool, Everton, Arsenal, Southampton

I suppose if you are in a World Cup-winning side with your 21st birthday still to come it is not easy to improve on that. But even if Alan Ball did not improve on the achievement, he certainly matured as a player of great distinction.

That should not have surprised anybody.

Alan Ball in his Arsenal days.

Opposite **Ball evading a tackle.**

It was so obvious during that 1966 World Cup triumph that he had talent to go on and become an exceptional·player, and at that time he had unlimited energy to compensate for any mistakes that may have arisen through inexperience.

Yet to understand Alan Ball as a player it is necessary to realise his physical attributes and limitations. He was no more than 5ft 6in tall and never weighed as much as 11st. But in the terminology of the old-time managers he had a first-class motor.

He could run all day if he wanted to, and through 90 minutes of any football match he played in he usually did run, and run, and run.

Why? Simple. He just could not stand being left out of what was going on.

Not only did he want the ball himself, when he could not have it he sought to guide others along the right path with non-stop and nearly always accurate advice.

It would not require an Olympic coach to discover that Alan Ball was never going to win a hundred metres sprint. He has never been blessed with pace. Consequently, he always had to develop his game according to his physical make-up, and whatever he may have lacked in sheer speed he always compensated for by quickness of thought.

Ball was always way ahead of the play. He read the game well, and read it quickly. The ball went away almost before it reached him.

He never could, it seemed to me, understand why other players made it look difficult when the game was so simple. He never touched the ball twice if once was enough.

Ball was accused of having a fiery temper. I do not agree with that. It was sheer competitiveness inherited from his father, Alan Ball senior, who played for several League clubs without achieving stardom and was determined that his son would succeed where he failed.

It was this competitiveness which brought Alan junior captaincy of most clubs he played for and even England itself.

Born at Bolton in 1945, Ball was given trials by the local club but was rejected on the grounds that he was too small. That hurt, but eventually he was taken on the ground staff at Blackpool. At last, he was on his way, and to a grateful father who had once made him play for Ashton United in the Lancashire Combination, a hard semi-professional competition, at the tender age of 14, he promised he would play for England before he was 20. He made it with three days to spare.

Before that he turned professional on his 17th birthday, made his First Division debut in 1962, and was a regular face in the senior team by the time he was 18.

Six weeks after winning his World Cup medal, which he immediately gave to his mother, Ball moved to Everton. Manager Harry Catterick paid £110,000 to break the then British transfer record. Ball, who had started as a right-winger, had then found his true position in the middle of the field.

Ball and Everton, whose captaincy he took over from England centre-half Brian Labone, went from success to success. Everton won the League in 1970, invariably finished high in the table in other years, reached one FA Cup final and the semi-final twice. And by the time Ball was 26 he had more than 50 England caps behind him.

Then, in December, 1971, Harry Catterick, the man who had once said that he would not sell Ball for a million pounds, sold him for £200,000, breaking the British transfer record again.

It was Arsenal who bought him. Though soccer's grapevine had been busy for weeks hinting that relationships between Catterick and Ball were not as good as they had been, the sudden move shocked not only the Goodison Park fans but most of the Everton players as well.

Arsenal had won the Football League title and the FA Cup only six months earlier. Why did they need Ball? Bertie Mee, then manager at Arsenal, believed that when a player of Ball's ability and character came onto the transfer market, quality was cheap at almost any price. And he was right.

Ball gave Arsenal a dimension they had been lacking. But unfortunately for them, some members of the double team began to go off song. There are those who believe that the side was broken up too quickly. Whatever the reasons Ball, though giving his usual 120 per cent, was unable to drive Arsenal to the heights Everton had achieved under his captaincy.

As long as Sir Alf Ramsey was England's manager the caps kept coming in. But Don Revie, after giving him the captaincy, dropped him, and that was the end of an illustrious international career.

Ball, a man of strong words and strong football principles, was always his own man. Differences followed when he thought Arsenal were not playing it the way they should. Ball was at issue with authority again, and it ended with him leaving Highbury for Southampton who were then in the Second Division.

The little man with the big name was on the way down, it seemed. But Ball vowed he was going to Southampton to win them promotion, and this he did at the end of the 1977-78 season.

Southampton's Lawrie McMenemy was a manager he could go along with, Ball said. They talked the same language. McMenemy made Ball captain and Southampton were back in the First Division with Ball the father-figure to a highly promising young team.

Responsibility always made Ball a better player.

Gordon Banks

England, Chesterfield, Leicester City,
Stoke City, Fort Lauderdale

At his peak, which by common consent was during the 1970 World Cup finals in Mexico, Gordon Banks was the best goalkeeper in the world.

As far as most First Division forwards were concerned, he had become the world's

Banks of England shows the ball to Yorath of Wales.

No. 1 four or five years earlier, and not many of us who played against him and watched him regularly in later years will disagree with that assessment.

Banks will live on and on in football history on the strength of that one great save from Pelé in Guadalajara which the whole world sees again, and again, and again. But probably the biggest compliment he can be paid is to suggest that he did not need to make that particular save to be confirmed as the world's best.

The inclusion of Banks in the England team had the effect of adding an extra man. Not only was he the goalkeeper, but he added a first-class footballing brain to the team's assets. Everybody in the side felt that as long as 'Banksy' was there all they had to do was concentrate on scoring goals. Gordon would sort out the other end.

Banks had so much confidence in himself that it overflowed into other members of the side. It was a confidence born of practice. Banks worked and worked at his game. Peter

Shilton, who followed Banks into the Leicester and England teams, has said that he was amazed, when he went to Leicester as a youngster, just how much Banks put into his game.

Certainly many a striker who has played with Banks has been grateful for tips based on the goalkeeper's knowledge of angles.

Nobody ever organised the defence in front of Banks. He did it himself and would not stand for anybody else interfering. Such was the respect accorded him that generations of colleagues did what they were told.

When I was playing for Fulham we used to look forward to the games against Leicester. Strangely, Gordon never seemed to play very well against us. But in subsequent years I began to realise that those were about the only mistakes he was making during a season.

Banks was the ideal build for a goalkeeper. At an inch over 6ft tall and weighing $13\frac{1}{2}$ stone, he could look after himself and most opposing forwards who fancied taking him on.

He had a very safe pair of hands and his judgement of when to come out and take a cross was perfect. His temperament was marvellous. Nothing ever bothered him. Nothing seemed to anger him. He had the great gift of amiability which soothed many an anxiety-ridden dressing-room.

It was one of the game's great tragedies that his career was finished by the loss of an eye in a car crash, because although he was heading for his mid-thirties then, Banks could have gone on for a number of seasons.

His record of 73 caps may be beaten. But not until another goalkeeper dominates the game for ten years as he did.

Banks was born just outside Sheffield, but both United and Wednesday missed him and it was Chesterfield who gave him his first paid contract. Chesterfield have a

Gordon Banks, whom many thought 'the best goalkeeper in the world', jumps to catch a high ball.

history of producing fine goalkeepers and they soon realised that they had done it again.

He spent barely 12 months there before Leicester took him as a teenager and he stayed at Filbert Street until 1967 when he was transferred to Stoke for £52,500, then the record fee for a goalkeeper.

Little more than a year earlier Banks had been voted the best goalkeeper in the 1966 World Cup finals. He was in his prime at 28, and was hurt by Leicester's decision to release him.

Their problem was the rising young star, Peter Shilton. Shilton was then only 17 and he or Banks would eventually have to go. Leicester opted to keep the younger player and collect the money for the older.

So Banks went off to Stoke, who had tried to sign him 18 months earlier, with his new chairman commenting that while people were running round spending £200,000 on players who might knock the goals in, they had just bought somebody who was certain to keep them out, for a quarter of that sum.

When Banks arrived, Stoke had a history stretching back more than 100 years, but they had won nothing. Gordon's impact was almost immediate. Stoke reached two semi-finals of the FA Cup, losing to Arsenal each time, and in 1972 a major trophy was won at last. Stoke beat Chelsea at Wembley to win the Football League Cup. To get there Banks had had to save a penalty from his England colleague Geoff Hurst three minutes from the end of extra time in the semi-final against West Ham to keep Stoke in the competition.

The car crash finished Banks as far as top-class English football was concerned. Stoke took him on their coaching staff for a time, and then he went off to the United States to excite a whole new generation of fans by playing for Fort Lauderdale.

Great nineteenth century footballer, Billy Bassett of West Bromwich Albion, a fine club servant.

William Isaiah Bassett

England, West Bromwich Albion

For more than half a century the name of Billy Bassett was synonymous with West Bromwich Albion. Indeed, I can think of few players in the history of the game who contributed more to one club in loyalty, affection and inspiration than Bassett. He was born in West Bromwich and joined the club in 1886 when he was 17 years old. He played for Albion until the end of 1899 and then turned his attentions to a business career. The directors of Albion elected him to their board in 1905 and three years later he became chairman. He held this post until his death in 1937. When he completed 50 years with the club he was presented with a silver casket by his colleagues.

Bassett stood only 5ft 5½in tall but he compensated for his lack of inches by his quick-witted play on the right wing. He possessed that hall-mark of all great wingers, an ability to keep the ball close to his feet, and he enjoyed nothing better than keeping to the touchline, making the corner flag his first objective. Once there he would cross the ball with such pinpoint accuracy that often the final scoring shot or header was merely a formality.

Albion have always achieved more success in Cup competition than in League commitment and Bassett was a member of their first FA Cup-winning team in season 1887-88. He had not played in either of the teams which lost in the previous two seasons to Blackburn Rovers (whose victory was their third in succession, a feat never since repeated) and Midlands' rivals, Aston Villa.

Albion were so determined to make it third time lucky that they prefaced their notices for their matches that season with the motto 'Death or Glory'. Even so, after a brave run to the final, Albion were scarcely fancied outside their own confines to beat the so-called 'Invincibles', Preston North End, who had scored 50 goals on the way to this game at Kennington Oval. Moreover, supporters of Preston could point to the fact that their side had achieved a run of 43 consecutive victories. Out of their bubbling confidence was born one of the Cup's most famous stories.

Chroniclers of the time reported that Preston felt so certain of the outcome that they asked the referee, Major Francis Marindin, if they could be photographed holding the trophy *before* the kick-off. Marindin is said to have replied, a trifle acidly: 'Hadn't you better win it first?'

How right he was! The records show us that Albion, whose wage bill amounted to just £5 10s, won a thrilling game 2-1 with goals by 'Spry' Woodhall, who played on the right wing with Bassett as his inside partner, and centre-forward Jem Bayliss, another who gave wonderful service at the Hawthorns.

By 1892, when Albion reached the final again, Bassett was established on the wing and he provided the centres for two of the goals in the 3-0 win over Aston Villa which thoroughly avenged the Cup defeat by their neighbours five years earlier.

Altogether Bassett made 262 appearances for Albion, a remarkable number when one considers how few matches were played in those formative years of the game. He won

16 caps for England, the first in a 5-1 win over Northern Ireland in Belfast in March, 1888, and, astonishingly, made eight consecutive appearances against Scotland.

Cliff Bastin

England, Exeter City, Arsenal

Until the mid 1960s when they became flank strikers, wingers knew their place. It was straight down the touchline, and the tactic was simple. They crossed the ball from the goal-line, and the centre and inside-forwards did the rest. Nevertheless, if a winger saw the occasional goal chance he was expected to take it.

One who took his chances was Cliff Bastin. In one amazing season, 1932-33, he hammered in 33 goals, still a record for a winger and likely to remain so for all time.

A softly-spoken Devonian who shunned

Bastin acclaims a goal for Arsenal against Huddersfield, Highbury, January 1937.

16

the limelight off the field, Bastin had achieved a striking rate of 157 goals in 367 First Division matches by the time he retired, and was universally accepted as the best of English wingers in the 1930s.

Even as a teenager, he demonstrated remarkable coolness. Part of it was due to deafness but most of it stemmed from complete confidence in his own ability.

Like Cliff Jones in a later era, Bastin was essentially a goalscoring winger. His left foot could be devastating, and the link he forged with Alex James, the inside-left of the baggy shorts, produced a conveyor-belt of classic goals during the heady 1930s.

James' forte was the searching diagonal pass. Bastin fed hungrily from them. He would linger ten yards in from the touch-line, collect James' offerings on the run and cut in for goal. It was simple, but so very effective.

Although he will always be remembered as a left-winger, Bastin started his soccer life at inside-left. He played 17 games for

The most prolific of goal-scoring wingers, Cliff Bastin of Arsenal.

Exeter in that position before joining Arsenal in the summer of 1929. He was 17 years old, and inside a year he became the youngest man ever to win an FA Cup medal.

It all began quietly, however. Herbert Chapman, then the Arsenal manager, picked him at inside-left against Everton and Derby at the outset of the 1929-30 season. He took some punishment from tough First Division defenders, and after just these two games, the precocious Cliff was in the reserves.

It was some months later that he re-emerged at first-team level, in the outside-left position in which he was to become famous. Cliff had apparently been surprised to the point of alarm when Chapman had told him of the positional switch. In retro-spect, though, it was a stroke of genius.

By the time he was 19, Cliff Bastin, who became known as 'Boy' Bastin, had little left to win in the game of football. The League Championship and FA Cup had both come to Arsenal, and Cliff had made his inter-national debut – albeit an unimpressive one – for England against Wales in 1931.

The honours just kept coming. Arsenal lorded it through the 1930s, winning the League five times in eight seasons and reach-ing the Cup Final three times in seven.

Bastin became a left-wing legend, making only occasional and nostalgic returns to his old inside-left territory when the masterful influence of James was missing through in-jury. One such occasion was the 1932 Cup Final, and although Bastin orchestrated the move from which Arsenal went ahead, the Cup went to Newcastle.

When the war intruded, Cliff had played almost 350 League games for Arsenal, scor-ing 150 goals. He had worn the England shirt 21 times for 12 goals – an impressive scoring rate for a striker these days.

His increasing deafness kept him out of the active services and he played regularly for Arsenal during the war years. A little surprisingly, he played only six times when League football resumed, before announc-ing his retirement at the age of 34.

Franz Beckenbauer

West Germany, Bayern Munich, New York Cosmos

Kaiser Franz. Was he the last of the attack-ing centre-halves? Or the first of the liber-ated sweepers? The real answer, of course, is neither. Beckenbauer, at his peak, was a footballer apart.

He was the prototype. There may be others of his kind to come. But in the early 1970s, and particularly when leading West Germany to victory in the 1974 World Cup finals, he was unique. There just was no other player comparable.

Beckenbauer was such an outstanding footballer in every respect that probably all but the experts regarded it as a waste to play him so far back. But advocates of that theory forget the agility of his football brain.

The ability to read the game and to think ahead meant that he could organise the game from the back. The natural leader in Beckenbauer functioned best when, chess fashion, all the pieces were out there in front of him. That is why he very rarely needed to tackle. Nearly always, simple interception was enough. And simple it looked, when Beckenbauer performed.

Then would come the killing burst up-field, a tactic born because neither West Germany nor Bayern Munich could afford to waste the rest of what he could do.

He probably achieved as much in terms of destroying the opposition by breaking up their rhythm and catching them by surprise five or six times in a game as lesser players did over the whole 90 minutes.

Attempt to mark Beckenbauer for pure skill and it must be ten out of ten, and I doubt whether anybody has ever passed better with both feet.

With his gifts and talent, Beckenbauer could play anywhere, and has. As a school-boy growing up in Munich, he was a

Franz Beckenbauer on the ball in a match against Chile.

traditional centre-forward capable of a hundred goals in a season. It was inevitable that he went through the Bayern youth teams, but it was as an outside-left that he made his Bundesliga debut in 1964.

By the time he was 19, Beckenbauer was in the West German squad preparing for the 1966 World Cup finals in England, having drifted back into midfield to give his remarkable creative abilities full rein.

The Germans, of course, faced England in the final and here Helmut Schoen, the manager with whom Beckenbauer enjoyed such close rapport, made one of the most controversial decisions of his career.

Schoen saw Bobby Charlton as the biggest menace to West Germany. He wanted him marked out of the game. And he gave the job to Beckenbauer, so robbing the side of their most inventive player's flair.

Eventually, after so much time in midfield, Beckenbauer got the job he wanted. He began sweeping, and gradually the face of West German football changed. They had won the World Cup in Switzerland in 1954 by running harder and stronger than any other team. In England in 1966 that was still their style, though slightly modified.

Came the revolution and by the time they were in Mexico for the 1970 finals the Germans possessed the best footballing team they had ever had. They should have been beaten by England in the quarter-finals but a goal by Beckenbauer, surging forward on one of his famous lightning strikes, became their lifeline. Germany might easily have gone on to face Brazil in the final had Beckenbauer not had to play most of the semi-final against Italy with an arm in a sling after injury.

Beckenbauer's big moment came in his native Munich in 1974 when he took the World Cup on behalf of a victorious German team that had given Holland a goal start in the first minute of the final.

Beckenbauer's proudest moment – holding West Germany's World Cup aloft in 1974.

There was no doubt as to who was the biggest name in the tournament. With Pelé gone, the title of the world's No. 1 footballer was up for grabs. It was either Johan Cruyff or Franz Beckenbauer and in 1974 it would have been a brave man who would have nominated one against the other.

A few years later, New York Cosmos needed a big name to follow the retiring Pelé and maintain the impetus of the American soccer boom. Cosmos went for Beckenbauer with such financial inducements that he had to give up the chance of playing in a fourth World Cup finals in Argentina in 1978.

Nobody could blame him. It was virtually security for life. But when he got to New York Beckenbauer found that he had to put the clock back and play orthodox midfield again.

The method of playing the sweeper's role that he had perfected in Germany was found to have a flaw. It could only be operated among players of top quality. The style was too sophisticated for Cosmos.

If Beckenbauer had to be summed up in one word, then that word would have to be elegance. It was with some sense of surprise that you realised that he had actually sweated through a game.

George Best

Northern Ireland, Manchester United, Stockport County, Fulham, Los Angeles Aztecs, Fort Lauderdale

There was a time when George Best had it in him to become probably the greatest player

George Best, despite all his skill, still a hard man in the tackle.

the world has ever known. The tragedy is that he did as much as anybody to create the off-field pressures he failed to live with.

On the field he really could be a superstar. Time and again he produced pieces of football skill that were sheer brilliance, breathtaking to see.

It might have been all so different if he had had the opportunity of showing the world what he could do at the highest level, the finals of the World Cup. But during his spell at the top, Northern Ireland failed to qualify for the last stages. If he could have paraded his skills to a worldwide television audience the acclaim that would undoubtedly have come his way may have banished a lot of the frustration he felt.

While there is hardly anything that can be done with a football that Best could not do better than most, he had one supreme quality.

That was tremendous acceleration. There was nobody in football boots who could move as fast as Best from a standing start. Add the agility and dexterity which threw most opponents off balance, and Best became uncatchable.

Towards the end of his career in England he lost some of this electric pace and it says a lot for a fine football brain that he was able to make a major contribution in other ways that did not depend so much on speed.

Best did it all so easily, and apparently instinctively, that too many fans thought his brains were in his boots. Nothing could be further from the truth. It just took Best longer than most to realise that football is a team game.

He had the true artist's appreciation of his own talents, and I have a feeling that most of us only saw the half of it. Best, in the close confinement of a five-a-side training pitch where players are always on top of each other, pulled some unbelievable tricks with

George Best playing for Manchester United in 1971 against Fulham, later to become his last British club, as he alternated between England and America.

a ball, if his Manchester United colleagues are to be allowed their contribution to the Best saga.

He was a marvellous dribbler. It was nothing to see him leave four, five and sometimes even six, men standing. Or falling, off balance. For a man of 5ft 8in, who when he was properly fit, weighed only a few pounds over 10st, he packed a powerful shot.

Thick neck muscles enabled him to head a ball as well as the bigger men and he was strong enough to look after himself when the going got a shade tough, as it often did with him.

Perhaps a slight weakness, particularly in his younger days, was a tendency to hang on to the ball too long. But he was very conscious that he was the entertainer; he was the player the fans had come to see.

Later, when he lost some of his pace, he had to bring his colleagues into the game and maybe he became a better all-round player for it. In this facet of the game, involvement with his team-mates, he was never on the same wavelength as Johann Cruyff. But then, Cruyff could not dribble like Best.

One of his Manchester United teammates once said after they had won a match without Best in the side that the reason for the good performance was that they had had a chance of playing with the ball.

Yet there were no complaints when the teenage Best, in a European Cup quarter-final tie at Benfica, put United three up in the first quarter of an hour by scoring twice and making another. Manager Matt Busby had ordered United to play a containing game in the first 20 minutes.

Best eventually became disenchanted with football and there lies the cause of his apparent disrespect of law and order. Best and referees did not get on. His disciplinary record was bad, but most of the offences were arguing and disputing with referees.

Best always insisted that he never got the protection to which he was entitled. It was not that he lacked courage. Certainly no-one can ever doubt that. But he resented the fact that he could always name a dozen defenders who would be ready to kick him.

Best grew up in Belfast, the son of a shipyard worker. He joined United at 15, returned to Ireland homesick after only two days in Lancashire and was immediately sent back. That was probably the most significant decision his father ever made.

By the time he was 17 he was making his debut in United's First Division team in 1962 and was rarely out of it when he wanted to play.

He was the new sensation. He was capped for Northern Ireland against Wales when he was only 17. In 1967-68 he was British Footballer of the Year, and the following December was European Footballer of the Year. Best was no more than 22, and already there was a sizeable fortune building up from commercial activities off the field.

While he was on the way to making a fortune, he was becoming public property. Eventually, the goldfish bowl life-style was to break him. Twice he announced his retirement and came back. But in 1973-74, the season Manchester United were relegated from the First Division, Best had had enough. He was only 28.

When United eventually gave him a free transfer, he came back to play a few games for Stockport. Then he had two spells at Fulham between wrangles over his contract, concerning whether his parent club was Fulham or Los Angeles Aztecs.

In the autumn of 1977, he decided his future lay in the United States and returned to Los Angeles. The decision was probably the right one. The glare of the limelight is not so fierce out there, and neither is the tackling.

But George Best, at his best, was a truly great artist who left an indelible mark on the minds of all who saw him.

Roberto Bettega

Italy, Juventus

It is not given to many players to suddenly break into world class rating at the ripe old footballing age of 27. But that's what Juventus striker Bettega did in the autumn of 1977 when, in a qualifying match for the World Cup finals in Argentina, he rammed four goals past a Finland defence, totally and completely unexpectedly as far as the rest of the soccer fraternity was concerned.

Cards marked, most of us then realised that the man who had played so intelligently for Italy against Don Revie's England side in Rome in November, 1976, had it in him to be one of the emergent names when considering whom the 1978 World Cup was

World Cup qualifying match, Rome, 1976, and Roberto Bettega flies through the air to head the second Italian goal against England.

likely to throw up as a natural successor to West Germany's Gerd Muller as the striker everybody feared.

Bettega had, in fact, been around for quite a time with Juventus but he had contracted an illness that put him out of the game for a long spell.

Out of sight and out of mind, he had gone quietly on loan from Juventus to Varese after being restored to fitness. Back he came, and then he and Juventus started complementing each other.

Italian team-manager Enzo Bearzot could not leave him out of the squad, and by the time he had completed a dozen international matches he had scored 13 goals.

That was a striking rate that put him well on course to eclipse all the Italian scoring records including those achieved by Boninsegna, Riva, Mazzola and the other stars of the 1950s and 1960s.

Bettega bears comparison with Riva in one respect only. Both are left-sided flank strikers. But where Riva was stocky and powerful, Bettega is slim. Where Riva took himself through a defence by sheer power and bombarded shots, the more slight Bettega threads his way through and tucks the ball away neatly. Bettega also has the gift of appearing to be coasting, until the ball is within playing distance. Then there is the burst over the first few yards which distinguishes the great from the good.

Bettega is also a menace in the air. With Bettega in the side, the Italians could afford to plan a British-style build-up with the ball being floated over the heads of the backs.

Bettega's anticipation, plus the neatest forehead in Italian soccer, were quite capable of doing the rest.

Danny Blanchflower

Northern Ireland, Glentoran, Barnsley, Aston Villa, Tottenham Hotspur

Danny Blanchflower was more of a captain than a footballer, but that does not mean he was not an outstanding player. His greatest

Bettega challenged by England's Roy McFarland.

stock in trade was his infectious confidence.

From the first moment he kicked a ball Danny had no doubt at all that he was great. That confidence, carried over into his play, would bluff and double bluff his opponents.

Fear played no part of his game. He always felt that attack was the best form of defence and in view of the entertainment his teams provided and the results they got who is to say that he was wrong?

In the old style of football the wing-half was supposed to mark the inside-forward and I remember playing against Danny when he was at right-half. He had the confidence to take the initiative and I spent the whole game running after him instead of the other way round.

He was a beautiful passer of a ball, very perceptive in the middle of the field and never knew when he was beaten.

He was a most deceptive-looking player.

He appeared fragile physically, but those legs could keep running for 24 hours a day if it were necessary to do so to get a result for his team.

Blanchflower was a thinker, not just a footballer. New and visionary ideas came easily to him, which is why he could not, in retrospect, have been expected to linger long in the Yorkshire backwater of Barnsley.

Danny was 22 when he joined Barnsley, hardly a tender age at which to break into English League football.

He had already served an apprenticeship – first by playing on the streets of Belfast with brother Jackie and even, occasionally, his mother, who had once played at centre-forward in a women's team. Glentoran had been his first club, and he will tell you now that he regrets his innocence in accepting a £50 signing-on fee and only £3 a match.

At least, though, Glentoran won him projection. In his opening season, he played for the Irish League against the Football

26

Blanchflower at the centre of a great Spurs team. Left to right, top: Baker, Henry, Brown, Norman, Smith, Jones. Bottom: Greaves, White, Blanchflower, Mackay, Dyson.

League. Two years later he was on his way to Barnsley for £6,000.

The move provided Second Division football for Blanchflower, but failed to provide the freedom for him to express himself. He played for Northern Ireland for the first time during his stop in Yorkshire – and lost 8-2 to Scotland – but early in 1951 he was on the move again, to Aston Villa.

This was more Danny's scene. Big crowds watched him; he was able to feel a major part of a major club. But still they would not listen to his theories.

Danny suggested that Villa should experiment with a 3-3-4 system that he had seen a Swiss side use. The idea was greeted with doubts if not scorn. In 1954, he asked for a transfer, Spurs and Arsenal led the bidding

and he went to the former for £30,000.

The love affair had begun, an affair that was to last ten years and make Tottenham one of the most successful and admired clubs in football history. Blanchflower was to be no mere cog in the machine – he was, as far as on-field matters went, to operate it.

Danny succeeded Alf Ramsey as club captain and immediately inflicted theories that were thought revolutionary on a team of willing ears. Well ... willing at first. When a Blanchflower ploy failed to produce results during the 1955-56 season, he was sacked as captain.

Northern Ireland now had Peter Doherty as manager, however, and here was a man truly on Danny's wavelength. He made him skipper and stuck by him unhesitatingly – with startling results.

They beat England in late 1957 – for the first time in 30 years. Then, against all logic, they not only qualified for the 1958 World Cup finals but fought through their group into the last eight, Blanchflower inspiring the decisive 3-2 win against Czechoslovakia. He was 1958 Footballer of the Year, and was to win the award again just three seasons later.

Bill Nicholson became Tottenham manager during the 1958-59 season and restored Blanchflower to the captain's job. It was an inspired choice, for together, these two were to make the club great.

The 1960-61 season is etched on the memory of every Spurs fan. Double year – the first club to win the League title and FA Cup together in the twentieth century. Tottenham strolled the League with 66 points, winning 31 of 42 matches. The Cup Final against Leicester was won 2-0.

Burnley were beaten in the next season's Wembley final, and Blanchflower apparently quenched his thirst for success with the 5-1 demolition of Atletico Madrid in the 1963 European Cup Winners Cup final.

By the end of the following season he had retired. He was not the same player now and Nicholson, sensing the inevitable, dropped him. Danny was too proud to languish in the 'stiffs'.

More challenges awaited him, too, in sports journalism, where he gained a reputation for outspoken attacks on soccer establishments – still thinking after all these years.

Ernie Blenkinsop

England, Hull City, Sheffield Wednesday, Liverpool, Cardiff City

Whenever people talk to me of England defenders between the two world wars, there

Classy full-back Ernie Blenkinsop clears the Sheffield Wednesday lines.

is a good chance they will include among their favourite selections, Ernie Blenkinsop. And in describing him they are likely to remind me what a *stylish* full-back he was in an era when one tended to believe that all backs were large, robust men whose creed was to thump the ball to safety.

Blenkinsop, in fact, was the very opposite of that image. He developed a remarkable sense of position which came about because he was such a good reader of play. Where other full-backs would be seen dashing onto the scene to make timely, if spectacular clearances, Blenkinsop seemed to arrive in the right place at precisely the right time, without flurry or fuss. Then he would transform defence into attack with a carefully-timed pass to a colleague in an open space. Everything he did laid the emphasis not on physique but on thinking.

In those far off days Sheffield Wednesday were a power in the land and Blenkinsop played a considerable part in the club's achievement of winning the League Championship in two successive seasons – 1928-29 and 1929-30, and Wednesday finished third in each of the next three campaigns.

During those heady days Wednesday also enjoyed the distinction of providing four players to the England team against Scotland in April, 1930 – Blenkinsop, Alf Strange, Walter Marsden and Ellis Rimmer.

Blenkinsop gained his first cap against France in Paris in May, 1928, and what a successful debut it proved, England winning 5-1 with 'Dixie' Dean scoring two of the goals.

He then proceeded to complete 26 appearances in succession in an international side which accomplished many notable performances, none more so, I suspect, than a handsome 5-2 victory at Wembley in 1930 over the Scots who two years earlier, and immediately before Blenkinsop's debut, had triumphed 5-1 with a team hailed in some quarters as the 'Wembley Wizards' and in others as the 'Blue Devils'.

Blenkinsop began his playing career with Hull and after service with Sheffield Wednesday, he moved on to Liverpool, finally bowing out of a game he had served so creditably with Cardiff City.

Oleg Blokhin

Russia, Dynamo Kiev

Generally, Russian football does not tend to throw up personalities. At least not unless they are goalkeepers like Lev Yashin or they have been around for ten years or so.

The exception is the highly mobile Oleg Blokhin, who made his debut for Kiev at the age of 18 and was a star of the 1972 Olympic tournament two years later.

Killing off the legend that all Russian footballers rely largely on brute force and

Oleg Blokhin, at 21 European Footballer of the Year in 1975.

bulk, Blokhin is a neat and tidy touchline performer mostly on his favoured left flank.

With ball skills that would not disgrace a Brazilian, Blokhin was Russia's Footballer of the Year in 1973 when he was 21. He won the award for the next two years and climaxed it all by becoming European Footballer of the Year in 1975, a very rare Russian to achieve such a distinction.

What Blokhin has going for him is a very smooth style. When he plays the ball away it flows. Blokhin and the big boot just do not go together. The format, the outlook, seems much more western than eastern Europe.

Blokhin is also a player who hates to be confined, always the hall-mark of an exceptional player. He scores from all positions along the attack as well as from his instinctive left.

He helped Dynamo Kiev achieve Russia's League and Cup double in 1974 and was instrumental in their retaining the League title.

The spin-off for Blokhin came when Russia decided that Dynamo Kiev, the most successful club in the country, would also become the national team.

Blokhin did not really need such a decision. He would have walked into any Russian national team.

Steve Bloomer

England, Derby County, Middlesbrough, Derby County

Whenever the legendary names of English goalscorers are discussed by those with long memories or an appetite for the historic performances of distinguished players, rest assured that Steve Bloomer's will figure in the conversation.

It has been said of boxers that it is the hungry ones who succeed. Steve was voracious in his desire to succeed in putting the ball in the back of the net. Perhaps there were occasions when his quest for goals made him selfish. Certainly he had his critics, despite his undeniable talents, but I

well imagine he could afford a quiet chuckle to himself when he read, in retrospect, that sometimes he ought to have been more of a team man. For after all Steve scored 352 League goals in 600 games in a career which began in 1892 and did not end until the First World War. Furthermore, he added another 28 in 24 internationals for England, and two more in a match against Germany in September, 1901, which was not rated as a full international. Steve was born in Cradley Heath in 1874 – ten years before his beloved Derby County was formed, and he made his League debut for County at Stoke in September, 1892. Those who saw that match must have wondered then if they were witnessing the arrival of a master marksman – because Steve scored twice in a 3-1 victory.

He remained with Derby until 1906 when

Steve Bloomer's total of 28 goals for England was a record till Nat Lofthouse beat it 49 years later.

30

he moved to Middlesbrough where in four years he scored 61 times in 125 appearances before a yearning to return to his first love took him back to the Baseball ground, which has been the 'Rams' home since 1894.

He continued to play until 1914 when he took a coaching appointment in Berlin where he had the misfortune to be interned during the First World War.

The records tell us that Steve scored 291 goals in 475 games for Derby but I have had to look elsewhere to discover what type of player, physically and technically, this scoring 'machine' was like. Old-timers tell me he was a slight and pale figure whose appearance was deceptive to those opponents who first faced him. But give him the ball and Steve would shield it with a possessiveness that evoked both admiration and despair from his challengers. When the goal came within his sights he was capable of sudden shots of immense power. Once, in a game against Sheffield Wednesday, in January, 1899, he scored six times. Nor were such individual feats confined to League games. In 1896 he was a member of the England team which went to Cardiff and thrashed Wales 9-1. Steve's contribution? Five from the inside-right position.

Indirectly Steve also played a part in the emergence of Italy as a World Cup power. Apparently Vittorio Pozzo, a driving force behind the Italian national teams in the 1930s, resided in England before the First World War and often discussed tactics with Steve. Clearly, he put the knowledge thus acquired to maximum effect because Italy won the World Cup in 1934, took the Olympic championship in 1936 and retained their world trophy in 1938.

Giampiero Boniperti

Italy, Juventus

Whenever I recall Giampiero Boniperti, my memory goes back to that October day at Wembley in 1953 when he turned out for the Rest of the World against England in a match to mark the 90th anniversary of the Football Association.

It happened to be Trafalgar Day and it required effort beyond the call of duty from the England players to preserve—at least until the Hungarians arrived a month later—their unbeaten home record against Continental opposition. The game was actually in its dying seconds when England, 3-4 down, were awarded a penalty after Stan Mortensen had fallen headlong in the area, and Alf Ramsey, seemingly unmoved by the tension of the occasion, calmly drove in the equaliser.

FIFA had gathered together magnificent talent from Austria, Germany, Italy, Spain, Sweden, and Yugoslavia and Boniperti was on the right flank of a forward line which also contained Kubala, Nordahl, Vukas and Zebec, supported by the sensitive probings

Boniperti (dark shirt) playing for the Rest of the World against England, and tussling with Alf Ramsey, 1953.

31

of Zlatko Cajkovski and Ernst Ocwirk.

Twice in a first half of superlative attacking skills Boniperti scored, first wandering into an unmarked position near goal to meet a cross from the left, then finishing off with almost arrogant efficiency a through pass from Vukas.

Those two moments crystallized for me the artistry of arguably the most successful forward to emerge from the immediate postwar years of Italian football.

Little wonder therefore that John Charles fitted into his role so effectively after Gigi Peronace had taken him from Leeds to Juventus in the summer of 1957. For on the one side he had the Argentian Omar Sivori and on the other the blond, adroit Boniperti, who had joined from Momo seven years earlier.

Boniperti made such astonishing progress that at the age of 19 he was given his first cap, against the Austrians in Vienna, but like others before him the occasion proved too much. Italy were trounced 5-1 and frankly Boniperti never had a proper opportunity that day to settle down. He was not called upon again for almost two years.

When he did return the circumstances were tragic because Italian football had just been deprived of eight Torino footballers, killed in an air disaster. But in an understandably emotion-charged atmosphere in Florence, the Italians defeated Austria 3-1 to avenge their previous failure. Boniperti, now far more mature, scored one of the goals and became an established international of considerable flair and vision.

Under his distinguished leadership Juventus achieved distinction in domestic and European competitions and it was a fitting climax to a remarkable career that he should become president of Juventus.

Josef Bozsik

Hungary, Kispest, Honved

The name of Josef Bozsik will always be closely associated with the great era of the

Hungarian national team of the 1940s and 1950s. During that marvellous period in their history the Hungarians went 13 years without suffering a home defeat – from the time of their 7-2 victory over Sweden in 1943 to their 4-2 defeat by Czechoslovakia in 1956 and reached the 1954 World Cup Final, losing 3-2 to West Germany.

Bozsik was a member of that team for most of those years and British followers will not easily forget his part in the sensational 6-3

32

The Hungarians brought a completely fresh and attractive approach to the game with each man running off the ball with tremendous adventure. I remember Bozsik's part in that performance. He was very much the organiser and provider of chances for those in front of him, quick to break up English raids and turn them into profit. He scored one of the goals and prompted several others.

Bozsik was born in Budapest and played for Kispest from 1937 to 1949 when that club became known as Honved. He remained with them as a player until 1963 – and then coached the club. Altogether he served Honved for more than 30 years.

He won a record number of 100 caps for his country between 1947 and 1962 and gained an Olympic winners' medal in 1952, but just missed fulfilling a lifelong ambition: to win a World Cup medal.

Hungary won their way to the final of the World Cup in Switzerland in 1954, only to lose 3-2 to West Germany, a match which ended his country's run of 29 games spread over four years without defeat.

After the revolution in Hungary in 1956, Bozsik was a member of the House of Representatives and he persuaded most of the Honved team which had been touring Spain at the time of the uprising, to return home. But Czibor, Puskas and Kocsis decided to stay.

In any assessment of Hungarian soccer, Bozsik is assured of a prominent place – and I, for one, will not forget his brilliant yet composed display that November afternoon at Wembley a quarter of a century or so ago.

Josef Bozsik (left) playing in the World Cup of 1958. He died tragically young while the 1978 finals were being played.

Billy Bremner

Scotland, Leeds United, Hull City

They do not come much smaller in stature and certainly no bigger in heart than Billy Bremner, a bubbling, bouncing package of football industry encased in a chalky white skin and topped off by a mass of flaming red hair. Bremner's enthusiasm and skill made

trouncing of England at Wembley in November, 1953, a game which ended England's so-called 'masters' hold over foreign opposition on their own soil. For, of course, that victory of the 'Mighty Magyars' was the first suffered by England against Continental opposition in their own land.

him skipper extraordinary of Scotland and Leeds.

Bremner began his illustrious career in 1960, out there on Leeds' right wing. When he finished it 18 years later after nearly a couple of years at Hull, it was surprising that there was any of him left.

For no footballer, surely, has ever run so far as Bremner whose passions for Scotland and Leeds were unique.

If Bremner did not have the ball, there was something wrong. So he went after it, affronted it seemed by the very idea that the game, any game, could actually be proceeding without his immediate involvement.

To state that Bremner was permanently hungry for the ball is an utter understatement. But it might explain why he was so deadly in the tackle.

Leeds' skipper Bremner keeping his eye on the ball.

There was only $10\frac{1}{2}$ stone of Bremner, but many are the opponents who have recoiled from a battling Bremner as if they have been hit by $10\frac{1}{2}$ tons! There was nothing subtle about a Bremner tackle or challenge, but there was about his passing. For a player with a hard-man label, his distribution was surprisingly fluent.

Nor was that the end of Bremner's talent. A midfield man for all but the very early days of his career, the little Scot threw in more than a hundred goals as a bonus. He had the knack, too, of scoring goals that turned big games.

His fearsome competitiveness sprang from a spartan upbringing in the Scottish town of Stirling. The young Bremner soon learned that if he wanted anything he would have to graft for it, and he has been grafting ever since.

Success on the field brought him the material things he had to do without as a boy, but comfort did not change his character.

He had trouble with his temperament. Back in Stirling he had to compete with bigger boys and sometimes men. There was only one way to go in – hard. Bremner, it seemed, could not change.

Then Leeds manager Don Revie played his master-stroke. He appointed Bremner captain, and that was the making of him.

Suddenly, an extra dimension was added to Bremner's game. Responsibility . . . to himself, to his team, and above all to Don Revie for having faith. Bremner repaid his debt with monumental interest, leading Leeds to most of their unprecedented triumphs in the 1960s and early 1970s.

The captain's job might have gone to Jackie Charlton, or shrewd Johnny Giles. But Revie got it right. Bremner's exuberance did not need subduing. It merely wanted harnessing and diverting into the proper direction.

The Bremner head, no more than 5ft 5in

Little tiger, big trophy. Billy Bremner with the Championship trophy, 1974.

off the ground, had to be used mainly for thinking, and Bremner realised he was heading in the wrong direction.

The power of Bremner did not alter. What he controlled was his own reaction to trouble, and his file in the FA's disciplinary office slowed its rate of growth.

By 1970 the reformation of Bremner was complete. He was Footballer of the Year and well on the way towards his 54 caps. He became one of Scotland's most-capped players, and big occasions brought out the best in him. Hampden Park and Wembley Stadium became his second and third homes.

To listen to Revie in praise of Bremner was to hear a monologue since Revie did not find many of his listeners in any mood to disagree.

Certainly not Scotland fans who rejoiced when his leadership took their country to the finals of the 1974 World Cup in Germany.

Bremner the man is as positive as Bremner the player, well able to look after himself and support opinions that are all his own.

Above all, he is a realist. When he started struggling to maintain his own high standard at Leeds, he moved down a division to Hull. And when the same circumstances overtook him there he retired from the game.

He might have adjusted to a less demanding position. He might have accepted that he could no longer control the game he was playing in and settled for something less exhausting.

But, being Bremner, he could not. And did not.

Charles Buchan

England, Sunderland, Arsenal

Charlie Buchan played only three seasons for Arsenal while he moved from the age of 33 to 36. Yet, historically, they were the most significant of a great career which should have been rewarded with far more England caps.

For it was Buchan, a traditional inside-right and one of the game's great thinkers between 1910 and 1928, who helped manager Herbert Chapman create the third-back defensive centre-half game and lay the foundations of the modern Arsenal.

Buchan, tall, long-striding, was an elegant player. And a spartan player, too. He wasted nothing, passes nor scoring chances. Buchan commanded his teams—he was a natural leader—like a captain on the bridge, with absolute authority.

He had all the makings of a fine manager. But after retiring on the day when Dixie Dean, of Everton, broke the League scoring record with 60 goals in one season, Charlie went to Fleet Street as football writer and broadcast regularly for the BBC.

Charlie was one of four brothers, three of whom went on to play professional football. Their father was a blacksmith in Woolwich Arsenal, which gave Charlie an early link with the club that was—one way and another—going to play a considerable part in his career.

By the age of 17, Buchan was playing in Woolwich Arsenal Reserves. He left after a petty row with manager George Morrell, over 11 shillings' worth of expenses.

Two seasons with Southern League Leyton followed. Then Sunderland spotted him, and in March, 1911, he was heading for Wearside.

It has been said that Charlie was so much a London lad that he needed a map to discover where Sunderland lay in England!

At first, the north-eastern public did not take to this spindly inside-forward who, at the age of 19, measured more than 6ft tall yet weighed less than 11st. Quite frankly, he was not strong enough for the big time.

Sunderland, however, groomed him well. Charlie gave up smoking and worked hard on his stamina. By the early games of 1912, he was in such impressive form that Scotland's management approached Sunderland to release the boy Buchan to play against England.

The club had to point out that, despite the

Scottish name, Charlie had been born in England. The fact that his parents were Scottish was not, in those days, enough to make him eligible.

This technicality delayed his international debut for only a year. In February, 1913, he took his place in the England side and scored their only goal in a disastrous 2-1 loss against Ireland – England's first-ever defeat against that opposition.

Two other Sunderland players were in the side with Charlie, and all three were dropped for the next international. Sunderland, as if to prove the national selectors wrong, went on to win the League Championship and reach the FA Cup final.

Wartime saw Charlie Buchan in the Grenadier Guards. It also saw the end of a fine Sunderland side. Buchan stayed at Roker Park for six years after the war, and was capped spasmodically. Then, in 1925,

Arsenal's new manager Herbert Chapman bought him in one of football's most ironic transfers.

The club which had allowed him to leave over an 11-bob argument 14 years earlier, now had to pay out handsomely to bring him back. Not just a transfer fee of £2,000, but also the pledge of £100 for every goal Buchan scored in his first season at Arsenal. He scored 21.

Buchan was a key figure – perhaps even deputy pioneer – in Chapman's revolutionary scheme to play a third full-back as stopper and draft one of the inside-forwards into a midfield area.

Who needs a ball? Bolton's Seddon and Greenhalgh (light shirts) in a ballet scene with Arsenal's Buchan. Goalkeeper Pym is out of step. Arsenal v Bolton, Highbury, 1925.

Charlie Buchan retired before Arsenal's greatest days dawned. All he could point to was an appearance in the Cup Final of 1927. But he was on the losing side again, Cardiff City taking the Cup out of England for the first time.

He was anything but orthodox. Sometimes, anything but elegant. Buchan was, however, a splendid passer of the ball, a prolific scorer and an effective all-round player. In 482 League games, he scored 258 goals, scheming many more. Yet for all that, he played only five times for his country.

Matt Busby

Scotland, Manchester City, Liverpool

Matt Busby came into League football in 1929-30, a right-half who believed that the ball should be coaxed and not crashed around the field.

Nine seasons later war broke out with Scotland's selectors having lifted their heads out of the sands but once.

Matt Busby in his playing days for Manchester City.

Sir Matt Busby was more famous as a manager than as a player. Here he is in his Manchester United office.

It took a war to get it right. Busby not only played in many wartime internationals during Army service, but as often as not his shrewd brain acquired the captaincy as well.

Busby the player was merely the prototype of Busby the manager. Calmly, completely in control, he possessed ball-skills not far short of the most gifted inside-forwards of his day.

He could dribble, but did not like to. He exerted his influence more as a reader of the game who preferred to make his killing with the one pass nobody, least of all the opposition, had any right to expect.

Like the popular music of that time, Busby's football was smooth tempo.

Busby's enormous success as a manager has tended to divert attention away from his qualities as a player. Do not be fooled!

He was born in 1909 in Bellshill, a small Lanarkshire village which also succeeded in producing the great forward Hughie Gallacher.

Like most boys of his generation in that area, he was the son of a miner. Matt, however, decided that the accepted tradition of pit life was not for him.

By the time he was 20, he was playing in Manchester City's League side – and impressing the fans with a flowing, accurate style of play at right-half.

Then, as ever, Matt was a charming man. But he had an edge to his game that could turn a match in a minute. He scored few goals – only 14 in a ten-year League career – but created many.

The pinnacle of his playing career was reached in 1934. The previous May, he had been in the City side which was destroyed, 3-0, by Dixie Dean and Everton in the FA Cup final. In 1934, they reached Wembley again. This time, it was their day.

Portsmouth provided the opposition and, with Busby at the hub of the City efforts, the Cup went to Manchester by a 2-1 margin.

Scotland recognised him at last. They picked him for the Home International against Wales but this was his only cap before the outbreak of war.

In 1936, after more than 200 League games for City, he was transferred to Liverpool. The club achieved little in his four seasons there, and when war broke out, Busby had reached the age of 30. The six-year interruption virtually guaranteed the end of his playing days, and he set about a new career within the game.

For 23 seasons, from 1946 to 1969, he managed Manchester United, first creating the Busby Babes and then rebuilding a team to win the European Cup, following the tragedy of Munich. In 1968, he was knighted, but nobody should forget that Sir Matt could play a bit, too.

Zlatko Cajkowski

Yugoslavia, HASK Zagreb, Partisan Belgrade

Back in 1953, when I was perhaps midway through my professional career, I was impressed by a man who paid his own fare from Belgrade to London to see the great Hungarians beat England 6-3 at Wembley.

I was more impressed when I discovered that he was Cajkowski, the great Yugoslavian wing-half who was then one of the great world stars, a footballer who played in the 1954 World Cup finals in Switzerland as well as those four years earlier in Brazil.

I remember thinking that if he still had something to learn about the game that justified that expense, then I had better stop considering that I knew most of it.

The gesture was typical of Cajkowski, who was destined to become one of Europe's foremost managers, particularly in eastern Europe.

As a player, he was back again at Wembley

Zlatko Cajkowski (10) scoring an off-side 'goal' against Sweden in the Olympic Final at Wembley, 1948.

a few months later as a member of the FIFA side that faced England, and there can be no higher praise than to suggest that he would not have looked out of place in the Hungarian side.

Nicknamed Tschik, he was an attacking wing-half of the traditional school, and his influence on the Yugoslav side can be assessed from the fact that he won 57 caps when there was nothing like the amount of international soccer played that there is now.

The great strength of Cajkowski was originality. He had a fertile brain and playing against him must have been a constant battle of wits that opponents usually lost.

He was a shop assistant in Zagreb when football beckoned, and he began a career which led to a string of domestic medals with the feared Partisan side from Belgrade. But who did most to make Partisan so respected? Cajkowski, of course.

Johnny Carey

Republic of Ireland, Northern Ireland, Manchester United

How well Carey would have fitted into the modern game, where inside-forwards come back and full-backs push up! For Carey was both of those in his time, and every other position on the field as well.

He was among the best all-rounders football has known, or is ever likely to know, and was the captain who inspired Manchester United to come from 2-1 down and beat Blackpool 4-2 in one of the really scintillating FA Cup finals.

Skill Carey had in abundance when he signed for United, his only first-class club, as an inside-forward. Style he added when moving back to wing-half. But when, after the war, he settled at full-back and added superb generalship to his game, then he became among the most gifted.

Carey took through his career the belief that in the long run the team that played

most football collected most of the plaudits. Manchester United's record between 1946 and his retirement seven years later, prove him so right.

Carey's statistics would be startling if for nothing else but the fact that he played for both Northern Ireland and the Republic of Ireland. What's more, he once played for them both in the space of three days, against the same opposition.

His career began through an accident. He was spotted by a Manchester United scout who had despaired of finding any talent in Ireland, yet decided to spend the weekend there. He went to watch a side called St James' Gate . . . and discovered Carey.

So it was, that, in November of 1936, Carey signed for United for £250. Cruelly split by the Second World War, his career never took him away from United, for whom he made more than 300 League appearances.

Carey's debut for United was in September of 1937, two months before he made his international debut in a Republic of Ireland shirt. His first season was also to end in a triumph, with United winning promotion back to the First Division, where they were to stay, with considerable success, for the rest of Carey's career.

At this stage, Carey was operating at inside-forward, and it could truthfully be said that he could have played anywhere on the field. His great days were still to arrive, however, and these were to come at full-back.

It was in the year immediately after the war that Johnny completed that unique three-day double, playing first for Northern Ireland, then for the Republic of Ireland, against England, at the end of September, 1946.

The following May, he captained the Rest of Europe against Great Britain. He could just as easily have been playing for Britain, who won the game 6-1.

This illogical situation had been brought about by the war years, in which Carey had left the Republic for good, and joined up

Johnny Carey, good in every position except goal, and superb at full-back.

with the British army. Soccer-wise, he was then eligible for both the North and South of Ireland, and neither forgot it.

The years following the war brought Carey's United their most memorable days. They won the 1948 Cup Final, despite trailing Blackpool 2-1 at half-time, and finished First Division runners-up four times in the five years between 1946 and 1951.

All the suffering of second-best was made worthwhile when the Championship came to Old Trafford in 1952. It was all Carey wanted to end his career, and after one more season, he quit the playing side of the game at 34 years old, and entered management.

Raich Carter

England, Sunderland, Derby County, Hull City

There might have been a cooler footballer than Raich Carter. It is doubtful, but arguable. What is beyond dispute is that I never saw a more confident player.

They used to tell a story about Raich pausing in mid-action to tug a comb from his shorts to arrange his silver hair back in position. It was not true, and it never could have been. Simply because the way Raich used to play, his hair never looked out of place.

Raich did not merely play in games. He ran them. They went the way he wanted. In his younger days, there was a turn of speed. Later, he did not need it. He would operate a few yards either side of the centre circle, and his voice carried the rest of the pitch.

He never seemed to move quickly. He waited for the ball to come to him. And it did. It might have been on a piece of elastic. Then the ball left Carter, still on the same piece of elastic, to reach a winger hurtling down the touchline some 30 yards away. Raich was still in control.

That was the illusion he created, this ice-

41

Horatio (Raich) Carter in pre-war Sunderland days, before his hair had turned to silver.

cool player who started with his native Sunderland in the early 1930s. He was an inside-left then, but without a flick of sweat switched to inside-right to become the greatest partner Stanley Matthews, in the England team, and Peter Doherty, with Derby, ever had.

Raich, for sure, would not argue with my assessment. As he saw it, there was nothing on a football field that he could not do. Most of the time he was right.

He could shoot, fiercely, with either foot. And in the days when inside-forwards were supposed to be goal takers as well as goal makers, he achieved a striking rate that brought him 216 goals in 451 League matches spread over 14 peacetime seasons. He won 13 England caps and would probably have trebled that but for the war.

He could kill a ball stone dead, with chest or foot. Perhaps he was not the greatest header of a ball I have seen, but Raich always argued that heads are for thinking with and that it's feet that play football.

He could dribble, but only if he had to. The real art of Raich was his ability to size up a situation quicker than most. Having moved into the open space, he always had time to do what he wanted with the ball.

As a rule of thumb, to tackle Raich meant arriving a second after the ball had gone.

He should have made an exceptional manager. He did not because the confidence that made him such an outstanding player became a handicap when he was a boss. Raich, the perfectionist, could not suffer fools gladly.

Average talent that could not improve offended his sense of propriety. It was not that Raich failed to appreciate his players' attempts to do better. He just could not understand why they found it so difficult in the first place.

Raich played for England as a schoolboy. Leicester gave him a trial and decided that he was not good enough. A few years later he was to become one of the youngest captains in the game.

In 1935-36 his enthusiasm, or arrogance, lifted a bunch of largely older players to win the First Division championship by eight points, and 12 months later he was skipper of the Sunderland team which beat Preston 3-1 in the FA Cup final.

Came the war, in which he served in the Royal Air Force, and after it Raich was rather surprisingly allowed to join Derby for who he and Peter Doherty had been playing as guests during hostilities.

Carter's defence-splitting passes helped Derby win the FA Cup at last in 1945-46 when they beat Charlton 4-2 after extra time.

Then the legs started to give out. In 1948 he joined Hull City, then in the Third Division (North), as player-manager and took them up into the Second Division.

He went to Leeds as manager, then on to Mansfield and finally Middlesbrough but never, at any time, did he look like producing a team that even remotely threatened to play as well as he did.

Raich Carter did not need a coaching manual. Soccer in the 1960s and 1970s has been living by one. So Raich and football went their separate ways.

John Charles

Wales, Leeds United, Juventus, Leeds United, Roma, Cardiff City

Big John Charles was a breathtaking player. He was 6ft 1in and 13st 12lb, and could balance and perform skills with the dexterity of a man half his size.

His perfect physique made him a handful for opponents whether he was at centre-half or centre-forward. When you added to his physique a full repertoire of control, passing, heading and shooting ability, then it all added up to sheer devastation in a football shirt.

This soccer package was wrapped up in such a soft, gentle personality that perhaps his true greatness was not properly appreciated during his career.

'The Gentle Giant' in 1957, the year Charles signed for Juventus and became 'Il Buon Gigante'.

The biggest problem he created for his managers was the decision where to play him. A fine football brain enabled him to read the minds of opposing forwards. Graft on that huge physique and you have a defence in itself. The temptation to play him there must have been great until the poor manager considered what he was throwing away as a striker. He used to put fear into the finest and the hardest of Italian defenders and there can be no higher praise than that.

Yet the amazing John, remarkably quick over the ground, could have been a graceful midfield player, too.

At the height of his Juventus days, he was the most idolised player in Europe. In Italy they called him 'The King'. Back in the Welsh hillsides the welcome was always for 'Big John'.

Was he the greatest Welsh player of all time? Difficult. But if you started picking Wales' Team of All Time, you start with John. And then wonder where to play him.

Born in Swansea in 1931, John joined the local Town club as soon as he was old enough. It was a romantic start, but one that was destined to last only as long as it took Leeds to spot his potential – and pay the princely sum of £10 for his services as an amateur.

In January of 1949, he was signing as a professional. Three months later came his League debut, at centre-half, and another 12 months passed before he won his first international cap and became the youngest man ever to play for Wales.

If all this happened in a rush, the next couple of years were relatively quiet for the 'Gentle Giant'. That all changed when the Leeds manager, Major Frank Buckley, decided to switch John to centre-forward for the 1952-53 season. It turned out to be one of the most inspired moves made by any manager.

Charles scored 26 goals in his first season as a forward. In his second, he set a Leeds club record and headed the full League

43

scoring list with an impressive tally of 42.

He was magnificent in the air, the terror of any centre-half. But he could not be ignored on the ground, where his strength carried him through so often—and I say strength advisedly, although he probably committed fewer fouls than any other player of his stature.

The turning point of his career arrived on April 19, 1957. It was, in any event, a significant day as John was captaining Wales for the first time. But, although the match itself was an unexciting and distinctly forgettable goalless draw against Northern Ireland, the presence in the Belfast crowd of a very wealthy Italian was to change the course of John Charles' life.

Umberto Agnelli was not only the president of ailing Italian League side Juventus, he was also high in the ranks of Fiat. Money was no object and, having liked what he had seen, Agnelli entered into negotiations with Leeds for one of the most momentous transfers in history.

The clubs agreed rapidly but John took longer to make his decision. Eventually, he signed in time to start the new season with Juventus. The transfer fee was £65,000, a record for a British player. Charles himself was promised fabulous terms.

Within a year, he was a hero in Turin, respected all over Italy. He could not walk down a street without seeing cafes empty of fans wanting to slap his back and shake his hand.

At first, he relished it all. A villa on the Riviera, another in Turin, a share in the ownership of a restaurant, two cars and the lifestyle of a film-star . . . or was it?

The press delighted in exaggerating, even inventing stories of Charles' lavish night-life. Inevitably, this led to an eventual conflict on two fronts—in his soccer and his home life.

Before that, however, he scored 23 goals

Centre-forward or centre-half, John Charles, in Leeds United strip in 1953.

44

as Juventus revived from gloomy times to win the Italian League in 1958. The following year they won the Cup, and in 1960 they achieved the Championship and Cup double.

Charles was also involved in Wales' drive to the World Cup quarter-finals in 1958, although he was absent when they finally went out to Brazil.

In April, 1962, Leeds paid £53,000 to have him back, but by September, with the disillusionment passed, John believed it had been a mistake to leave Juventus. He returned to Italy for ten brief and costly matches with Roma. His best, though, was blatantly past, and Cardiff had to pay only £20,000 when they signed him in mid-1963. It was perhaps fitting that he should end his League career where his life had begun . . . in South Wales.

Bobby Charlton

England, Manchester United, Preston

Bobby Charlton was an exceptional athlete as well as a brilliant footballer. He would have been a success at any game to which he really applied himself. For instance, I have watched him playing golf when he has hit the ball further even than Brian Barnes, a fact confirming that power just oozes out of him.

I remember seeing Bobby playing for England in his early days when he was out on the left wing. His sheer pace was almost out of this world. He would push a ball past his opponent and leave him standing in a yard!

In those days he was raw and inexperienced. Most of us were wondering what kind of player he would make when he began taking advantage of all the assets he had at his disposal.

We did not have long to wait, and when Bobby did begin putting it all together there was no better sight in football. The youthful surge and acceleration were still there, of course, but he had begun to learn

Bobby Charlton as most remember him – thinning hair, Manchester United shirt, beautiful control.

to slow opponents down. And, more important, he had learned how to slow himself down so that he was able to become a more cultured passer of the ball.

That achieved, the statistics, spell-binding, began to accumulate.

There was the World Cup winners' medal in 1966. The European Cup winners' medal in 1968. Three League Championship medals in 1956-57, 1957-58 and 1966-67. An FA Cup winners' medal in 1962-63. European Footballer of the Year in 1966. British Footballer of the Year, also in 1966.

And the small matter of 106 England caps and 49 goals.

Between 1956 and 1973 when he retired, he played 606 games for Manchester United and scored 198 goals. No wonder there is a special place for him in football history.

What made him unique? I would say it was his capacity at the very highest level, and that means the World Cup, to turn a game in an instant by scoring the kind of goal that nobody else on the park would be capable of scoring.

He did it for Manchester United when they took the European Cup from Benfica and he did it earlier for England on their way to World Cup glory. His ability to strike a ball accurately for goal with either foot in almost any circumstance was absolutely extraordinary. Shots did not just leave his feet. They exploded from the instep, and unless the goalkeeper was actually struck by the ball there was no way he was going to make a save.

Charlton found his true role in the middle of the field in time for the 1966 World Cup. But he was so many players rolled into one.

When he first came into the Manchester United side in 1955-56 he was an inside-forward. Right, left or centre, it did not seem to matter. He stayed around the edge of the box and just banged them in.

Then came the Munich air disaster which transformed him from fledging youngster to one of the senior professionals in a few minutes of horror.

He came back, found the game difficult, and moved out to the left wing. The 1958 World Cup in Sweden was played only a few months after Munich, and though Charlton was in the squad, he did not make the side.

He played a few more games as a striking centre-forward before making the outside-left position automatically his until the autumn of 1965. Then he started directing operations from midfield. He stayed the hub of England's tactical thinking for five years before bowing out after England's World Cup defeat by West Germany in Leon in 1970. Like most people, Charlton thought when he came off during that game that his next cap was only days away in the semi-final of the competition.

During those years of influence, Charlton was a bigger edition of Johnny Giles, with power.

If the Hallé Orchestra had moved down the road to Old Trafford, Charlton would have conducted them, too. He was perfectly able to slow the game down. He had by now mastered completely the art of screening the ball.

He could slot the ball from wing to wing, the massive power in his thighs giving him the gift of moving the ball instantly over 40 yards or so with very little backlift.

He had acquired the knack, or the experience, of strolling into the open space to pick up any ball played gently forward out of his own defence, or his opponents', too, if they grew careless.

He could spend the entire 90 minutes tantalising the opposition, but doing it all with absolute majesty and grace.

Yet, perhaps the most exciting facet of his play, the one which made crowds stop breathing, was his ability to surge past players at will, leaving them for dead. Those are the Bobby Charlton moments his fans will remember.

If a rival player, not stricken with panic, was courageous enough to make some sort of challenge, then Charlton could withstand it, and the surge would gather momentum. At the end, with chilling inevitability, would be the blockbusting shot.

With modesty, Charlton has admitted that the shot was as likely to hit the corner flag as crash into the net. But not very often, not very often.

I suppose it was the wide variety of skills and abilities that he had at his disposal that made him such a difficult player to cope with and so outstanding in his field. He

A measured pass, perfect balance—the maestro at work.

never looked to have to hurry, always he seemed to have time on his side.

That certainly was not the case for Manchester United when they signed him. There were said to be 18 clubs chasing the schoolboy star from Ashington in Northumberland. If Charlton's career did nothing else, it proved that 18 people cannot all be wrong.

The captaincy of Manchester United was naturally his, and most appropriately when the Old Trafford club won the European Cup for manager Matt Busby in 1968. Charlton also captained England.

When he retired, prematurely perhaps, in the spring of 1973, he became manager of Preston within weeks. He had a season on the less energetic but more nerve-wracking side of the touchline and then came back to play a few games.

But unlike most managers, Charlton did not have to rely on the game for a living. When Preston's directors interfered with a proposed transfer, Charlton made his point, and resigned.

He could afford to. The game had been good to him. But who could deny he had been very good to the game?

Ray Clemence

England, Scunthorpe, Liverpool

All great goalkeepers have the same outstanding attributes – marvellous reflexes, good anticipation, lots of courage, a large pair of safe hands, and a great kick to put opponents' defences under pressure.

Ray Clemence has all of these and more to spare. Above all, he is consistent. Just about the most emphatic tribute that can be paid to the Liverpool goalkeeper is that his mistakes are remembered longer than a string of magnificent saves.

That these mistakes number just two or three is quite remarkable when it is considered how much time he spends demonstrating his art in front of television cameras. Liverpool's tremendous success in recent seasons means that Clemence is one of the most over-exposed goalkeepers in the world.

Like good referees, exceptional goalkeepers are rarely noticed. They just go on making save after save. They can be taken for granted. They make it look so simple that it appears one of the easiest ways of making a living that anybody ever invented until, suddenly, comes the blinding save.

Clemence is such a goalkeeper. The way he plays he gives the impression he has never heard of the word flamboyance. It is only after he has made a truly exceptional save that the average spectator realises just how well Clemence has been playing.

Quiet off the field, Clemence is noisy on it, and that's another hallmark of the top-class goalkeeper. Clemence dominates his defence and he is right to do so. It is the only way.

Indecision gives away more goals than any any other fault. Clemence believes in letting his defenders, whether Liverpool's or England's, know exactly where he is and what he wants them to do.

Generally, Clemence goes about his job displaying all the goalkeeping skills without fuss or apparent flair. He is probably at his best in the situation most goalkeepers dread, when a striker breaks through the defensive barrier in front of him and Clemence has got to make up his mind.

Not whether to come out or not. Clemence always knows the answer to that one. But when.

The average goalkeeper, too often, is caught on his line. The striker is through before he realises the danger, and that is when you see goalkeepers jumping up and down on their line, dithering.

Not Clemence. He has probably seen the opening before the forward and without any hesitation he is sprinting out.

Less spectacular, but equally effective, is when a through ball pierces the defence. Clemence is out, quite unhurriedly, to collect it, absolutely without panic, before any opponent can get near.

He reads the game well. His timing is

superb. And his brain is cool. Once having gathered the ball, Clemence, as the modern game demands, becomes an attacker. He throws very intelligently and kicks very accurately.

In fact I wonder, sometimes, that perhaps the occasional error does not come because he might have been too quick in trying to size up attacking possibilities and consequently taken his eye off the ball too soon.

It all started for Clemence, who has won more England caps than any other goalkeeper except Gordon Banks, at Skegness, a seaside resort in Lincolnshire which isn't exactly a hotbed of soccer. He graduated from there to Scunthorpe in 1964. He had

Ray Clemence jumps to save for Liverpool.

A photographer behind the goal catches Clemence in action in an FA Charity Shield match.

played only one full season when Liverpool swooped.

It was a typical Liverpool signing, seeing a player of promise in the lower divisions and getting him to Anfield for a comparatively small fee.

Clemence, like many before him, found himself sentenced to reserve team football while he learned what the game, the Anfield way, is all about.

Two full seasons went by without the young Clemence getting a look-in. He had made up his mind that if he reached the end of the 1969-70 season without getting a break there was going to have to be a talk with manager Bill Shankly.

But Liverpool suffered the ignominy of an FA Cup tie defeat by Watford and Clemence at last was in. And Tommy Lawrence, the goalkeeper Clemence had understudied and then supplanted, never got back.

Clemence took his chance in the same style that he takes a ball – with both hands.

Alf Common

England, Sheffield United, Sunderland, Middlesbrough, Woolwich Arsenal, Preston

I suppose one of the first occasions I became aware of Alf Common's place in soccer history was during the negotiations I conducted for the Professional Footballers' Association on the abolition of the maximum wage. More than once the sports writers, in

that transfer. 'Boro defeated Sheffield United by a single goal and that was scored by Common from a penalty. It was his new team's first away League victory for almost two years and his skills as an inside-forward soon allayed fears that 'Boro might slip into the Second Division.

Common had also scored on his international debut exactly a year earlier when he was brought in at inside-right against Wales at Wrexham in a 2-2 draw. He was on target again in the following match in Belfast when the Irish were defeated 3-1, but he made only one further appearance for his country. That was in March, 1906, when he led the attack against Wales at Cardiff and England emerged victors by a goal to nil.

During season 1903-04 Sheffield United – his first club – boasted such a wealth of talent that as many as 12 of their players represented the country of their birth, among them Common. On occasions United were able to field 10 capped players in their

Today a footballer might cost £1,000,000. Alf Common caused a sensation when he cost £1,000 in 1905.

tracing the history of wages and transfers, recalled the first four-figure deal. And that, of course, involved the move of Alf Common from Sunderland to Middlesbrough in February, 1905, for £1,000.

We have all become so blasé at the astronomical sums paid for players in the 1970s that it is hard to conceive the impact which that £1,000 transfer had on the Edwardian administrators. They were so taken aback that a special commission was appointed to examine the circumstances of the signing. But after protracted investigations they had to admit that they found nothing sinister, no 'under the counter' arrangement which could shake the propriety of the era.

A few days after joining Middlesbrough, Common started paying back the cost of

League side. By today's valuation we should probably be calling them the £2½ million team. One of those internationals, incidentally, was the remarkable Billy Foulke who was reputed to weigh in excess of 20 stone – and he was a goalkeeper! Clearly a case of 'they shall not pass'. . .

Subsequently Common played for Woolwich Arsenal before Preston signed him in 1913 for a fee, this time, of only £250.

Warney Cresswell

England, Sunderland, Everton

South Shields, later to move to Gateshead and adopt that town's title, were struggling to make ends meet soon after the end of the First World War, when Sunderland were one of several clubs attracted by the talents of Warney Cresswell, a South Shields player. In March, 1922, after much heart-searching, the directors of South Shields accepted a fee of £5,500 from Sunderland –

Warney Cresswell (left) playing for Everton at Stamford Bridge in 1932. Hughie Gallacher is behind the fallen player.

a record sum for a defender at that time – and Warney was launched on a distinguished career in the First Division.

His calm and authoritative play at full-back had already earned him one international appearance while with South Shields – at right-back for England in a goalless draw against Wales at Cardiff in March, 1921. He wore the England jersey four more times while with Sunderland between 1923 and 1926 and played twice more – the last occasion in 1929, as an Everton player.

I remember Joe Mercer telling me how he went to Goodison Park as a 16-year-old starry-eyed boy and learned his trade from people like 'Dixie' Dean and Warney Cresswell. 'You could not have had better teachers than these two' said Joe, who obviously picked up a point or two . . . skippering Arsenal to Championship and Cup honours and taking Manchester City to the League title when he turned to management.

When the giants of the 1930s talk of Warney, they all seem agreed that what they admired most about his play was his com-

posure. You rarely saw him scrambling to rectify a dangerous situation. Such was his awareness of tactical ploys by opposing teams that frequently he was a move ahead in taking up positions to counter their attacks.

Not surprisingly he figured prominently in the two League Championships which Everton won during his nine years with them – in seasons 1927-28 and 1931-32. He also gained an FA Cup winners' medal at Wembley in 1933 when the 'Toffeemen' beat Manchester City (for whom Matt Busby was at right-half) 3-0.

His League career stretched from 1919 to 1936 and covered 569 League matches alone, a wonderful testimony to his dependability, skill and fitness.

His final appearance for England came in Belfast in October, 1929, when he was paired at full-back with Ernie Blenkinsop, and he had the satisfaction of helping to keep England's goal intact as the team won by three goals. Subsequently he ventured into management with Port Vale and Northampton Town.

Bob Crompton

England, Blackburn Rovers

Blackburn Rovers have provided many pages to the history of our game but none I vouch can surpass that which describes the dedication and marvellous consistency of their great servant, Bob Crompton. He signed for them in October, 1896 and remained with them until May, 1920. In that time he made 528 League appearances and gained 42 international caps for England.

As a player and subsequently director and manager, Crompton earned respect wherever he went, an object lesson to some modern-day stars who will be remembered for their playing skills and far less for their conduct.

Crompton did not lack physical attributes. In fact, he was ideally built to bowl over the wingers of his day, but that was not

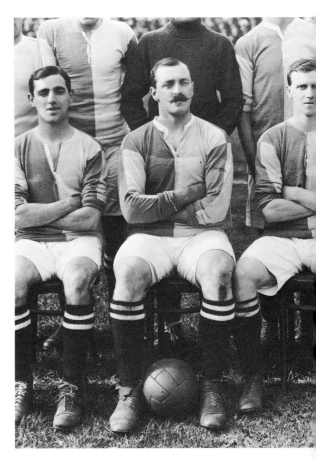

Captain of Blackburn Rovers and England, Bob Crompton was a fine military-looking figure.

Crompton's way of playing. Like other class full-backs he preferred the craftsman's approach – cool, unhurried and efficient, a combination which actively inspired those around him.

He missed only five of 45 matches for England between 1901 and 1914 and his record of 12 appearances against the 'auld enemy', Scotland, remains unchallenged to this day. Crompton, of course, was playing at a time when England were seldom called upon to play foreign opposition so that 34 of his internationals were in the Home International Championship.

Blackburn were great FA Cup exponents in the early years of the tournament and won the trophy five times between 1884 and

1891, but their greatest Cup days had passed when Crompton joined them, and he always missed out in his search for a Cup winners' medal.

In my researches I also noted that Crompton took part in the first official internationals between a home country and a foreign country. These were two pioneering matches against Austria in Vienna on June 6 and June 8, 1908. England won the first 6-1 and the second even more emphatically, by 11-1, and on that same European tour, an entirely new venture, they beat Hungary 7-0 in Budapest (where 46 years later the Hungarians were to gain ample revenge with a 7-1 scoreline in their favour) and Bohemia 4-0 in Prague.

After he gave up playing, Crompton briefly managed Bournemouth but he was essentially a Blackburn man and nothing probably pleased him more than being a member of the Rovers' teams which carried off the First Division Championship in 1912 and 1914, the only two occasions on which the title has gone to Ewood Park.

Johan Cruyff

Holland, Ajax, Barcelona

By the middle of the 1970s there was, for me, only one claimant to the title of being the greatest player in the world. Johan Cruyff, the Dutch master, was that man.

He combined just about everything that is good in the game. He was a marvellous

Johan Cruyff goes round Berti Vogts in the 1974 World Cup Final.

team man in that he could take part in combined play at the highest level. The passing could never be too quick for him nor too slick for him. How could it be? Most of the time it was Cruyff himself who was organising it. Shooting, dribbling, captaincy, defending, striking or whatever–name it and Cruyff could do it, with a lightning brain.

For when Cruyff plays it is chess at motor racing pace.

I rate the truly great modern footballer as one who can do the damage in his opponents' penalty area. I know that midfield control is important, and I appreciate that the artistry that goes on there is quite admirable. But anybody who calls himself a forward in this very crowded and tough defensive era has got to do his stuff where it counts.

Cruyff has never been afraid to dive in where it hurts, and that is what gives him the edge as an all-round player.

I think he is more of a natural leader than Pelé. The Brazilian had such natural ability. He was fantastic. But Cruyff is more of a student.

He knows the game from A to Z, and if the alphabet had any more letters he would know those as well. Everything for Cruyff starts from his brain. With Pelé it starts from his physique, and that is the difference between the two.

There have been times when Cruyff's considerable powers of leadership have not been appreciated, but not, I suspect, by those who have played alongside him.

He is a strong personality. From time to time, there were clashes with some of his Dutch team-mates. But he was so supreme compared with most of his colleagues that the best dividends came when Cruyff was left to get on with it, his way.

On the field he might have appeared arrogant. I prefer to think it was absolute confidence. Perhaps Cruyff himself believed he was the greatest. He certainly played like it. And was there ever any real point in disputing it?

When he moved from Ajax to Barcelona

he cost the Spanish club around £900,000, and pocketed a lot of that himself.

A shrewd judge of his own commercial value, Cruyff made his father-in-law his manager. And capitalised on the fact that one of the senior Ajax club officials was also one of Holland's leading tax experts.

But with a ball Cruyff could do his own talking. He was lucky in one respect. He was born with the gift of exceptional acceleration. Perhaps he was lucky too, to have been born with an absolute love for football.

Nobody, then, ever had to teach him ball control. His boyhood was spent with a ball at his feet and he had most of the skills by

This picture suggests Johan Cruyff's greatest asset–his speed off the mark.

the time he joined Ajax as a lad of 15. There was never any question of him going anywhere else because he had followed the famous Amsterdam club as a boy.

As a club, Ajax were to reach their peak during Cruyff's manhood. He won his first cap for Holland in 1966 when he was 19.

Seven years later when he went to Barcelona he was the superstar who had guided, cajoled and inspired Ajax to win the European Cup in 1971, 1972 and 1973. Barcelona, by their high standards, were struggling when he joined them. The following season they won the Championship proving that buying class is never as expensive as it looks.

Meanwhile, Holland were emerging as favourites to win the 1974 World Cup in Munich. But, how would they fare with Cruyff playing nearly all his football in Spain?

Dutch fans might have worried. Cruyff did not. All Holland had to do was play the way he wanted.

It is history now that Holland lost a final against West Germany that most non-Germans were expecting them to win. But defeat did not stop the Dutch being recognised as the most entertaining and individually skilful team in the tournament.

In his earlier days, Cruyff was quite a prolific scorer. He drifted just a little wider and a shade further back for the best of reasons. He was getting kicked too much.

The move improved his game. He saw more of the play and became far more influential. His ability to make the most accurate of passes over long distances meant that he could open up any defence, and given the space in which to operate he could still produce the devastating speed and change of pace that made him impossible to mark.

Cruyff, going wide, invariably took two defenders with him. Holland, Ajax and then Barcelona colleagues owed a lot of their goals to him.

But Cruyff himself, owed nothing to anybody. He was a self-made player in the same sense as Pelé and di Stefano. They were impossible to coach. You did not put Cruyff into a team. You built a team round him and that famous No. 14 shirt which superstition demanded he wore instead of a conventional number.

Bill 'Dixie' Dean

England, Tranmere Rovers, Everton, Notts County

The greatest of all time. Now there is a claim to make on behalf of any footballer. But in one aspect of the game, it was true of Dixie Dean.

Not as an all-round footballer, of course. That is too sweeping an assessment to make of anybody. But, defying the generation gap, he is still acknowledged, more than 50 years after playing his first League match, as the finest header of a ball in front of goal that the game has ever produced.

He was a centre-forward of the old school. For him, there was only one place to put the ball, and anybody who got in the way might well get hurt.

That is not to say that Dixie was a dirty player, or that he had no ball skills. He had. But he also had 12st of hard muscle on a 5ft 10in frame.

Dean, in full cry for goal, was a sight to behold. In 16 first-class seasons he became one of the few players to score over 350 League goals, and his grand total of around 500 included 18 in only 16 England matches.

Nobody counted in those days in the 1920s and 1930s, but it is accepted that around half of them came from his head. I'm told most of them went in like bullets.

Dean's achievements in the 1927-28 season are unlikely to be surpassed. It seems inconceivable now that any First Division striker should score 82 goals in one season — 60 of them in 39 League matches.

Yet Dixie's feat assumes superhuman proportions after what he went through a matter of months earlier.

His motor-cycle crash in Wales during 1927 stunned the city of Liverpool, rather as an accident to one of the Beatles might have done almost 40 years later.

He came out of it with fractured skull and jaw. He would never, the examining doctors announced, play football again.

But this was no ordinary mortal being written off, and he was back in an Everton shirt in time to start the most momentous season of his life.

It was a season in which forwards revelled in the new freedom created for them by the change in the offside law. The previous season, Middlesbrough's George Camsell had exploited the alteration to score 59 times for his Second Division club. Now it was Dean's turn.

He began with seven goals in the first three games of the season, dispersing any doubts over the extent of his recovery from the accident. With three matches left, he had gathered together 50 goals. Camsell's record seemed safe.

In the first two of those remaining games, however, Dean struck seven times. The final fixture was at Goodison, against Arsenal. Dixie needed a hat-trick—and got it in the most dramatic fashion imaginable.

Within minutes of the start, he had scored twice. But Arsenal fought back to equalise, and only 12 minutes were left when that famous head rose and forked forwards to butt in the match-winner and record-breaker.

The game adjusted itself and the stopper centre-half appeared on the scene. Dean, who was in any case big and powerful enough to break through on the ground, and agile enough to beat anyone in the air, countered quickly. He developed the ploy of heading the ball backwards or sideways, laying on goals for colleagues instead of attempting to score himself.

It was vastly successful, but did not preclude Dean from scoring plenty himself. By the time he left Everton to see out the twilight of his career at Notts County, he was

Dixie Dean, the best header for goal there has ever been.

within three goals of his final total of 379 in 437 League games.

Since retiring from the game, Dean has had an unsuccessful shot at running a pub and a long spell working for the Littlewoods soccer pools organisation.

In 1976, he had his right leg amputated. True to form, he recovered completely, and returned to his previous position as folk hero of Liverpool.

He was one of the very few sportsmen, or for that matter entertainers of any kind, who managed to capture the rapt attention, even idolisation, of the general public – before the television media made idols everyday creatures.

Dixie was a god in Liverpool and a respected hero to the rest of England.

He helped Everton win the First Division twice, the Second Division once and the FA Cup. His goals were the talk of each Saturday night; his head became a matter for legend.

Yet the irony of the man known to everybody following the game as Dixie, is that he could not stomach the name – and still cannot. He was christened William Ralph Dean. He was Bill to his friends. 'Dixie' just made him wince.

Kazimierz Deyna

Poland, Legia Warsaw
If the Frankfurt pitch had not been so waterlogged that the local fire brigade had to

be called in, then the World Cup Final of 1974 could easily have been between Poland and Holland instead of West Germany and the Dutch.

Poland, the shock team of 1974, were as close to the World Cup Final as that, and the man responsible was Deyna, a midfield player of tremendous skills.

The rest of the world might have been surprised at his sudden emergence. Englishmen and Welshmen who had played against the Poles in qualifying rounds were not.

Nor were those who had seen Poland perform in the Olympic Games soccer final in 1972 when Deyna, who packs a powerful right foot shot for a midfield specialist, scored both goals.

There are some players who know instinctively how the game should be played, and Deyna is one of them. See the Poland team playing and you know immediately who the boss is. He had not been able to rule the game when Wlodzimierz Lubanski, the Gornik midfield man and Deyna's colleague for Poland was in his prime, but after Lubanski's serious injury against England in 1973, Deyna achieved universal recognition.

Deyna simply assumes control. The middle of the field is his. He pulls all the strings in much the same way as Bobby Charlton did.

He and Charlton were completely different in style, but their effect on teams, in terms of influence, was remarkably similar. Colleagues had to respond to Deyna simply because he could do it all himself.

He was an immaculate passer and like every quality player was always looking for the killing ball. He had the ability to dictate the pace of the game. Then, suddenly, after

Left **Kazimierz Deyna is largely responsible for Poland's good runs in the World Cup finals of the 1970s, particularly 1974 when Poland finished third.**

Right **Kazimierz Deyna, the midfield master with the knack of scoring goals.**

some careful and deliberate play, he would unleash a ball that nobody else had seen as a possibility.

That was his real strength, the one quality that lifts him into the ranks of memorable players. Deyna had the capacity, more common in South American or Latin players, of screening the ball particularly well, and, an attribute of the complete midfield player, he could suddenly burst through and deliver a scoring shot.

Until the 1970s, Poland were very much a second-class power in world soccer ratings. They owe Deyna a great deal for their present eminence.

Didi

Brazil, Fluminense, Botafogo

The first of the great modern Brazilians to make an impact on the European soccer fans was Didi. He was in Switzerland for the 1954 World Cup when Brazil lost to Hungary in the infamous Battle of Berne and played in teams which won the World Cup for Brazil in Sweden in 1958 and Chile in 1962.

All the best Brazil teams have had a near-genius in midfield and Didi was the man of his time.

Though, like most Brazilians, he could look after himself if the going started to get a shade tough, Didi believed in football for its own sake. He saw it as an art form rather than a physical contest and to emphasise the point he had the Peru team, of which he became manager, playing that way in the 1970 World Cup in Mexico.

As a player, Didi wanted no part of defence. He ran the Brazil midfield cleverly, always seeking to keep the game moving, always able to reach any corner of the pitch with beautifully weighted passes with both feet. He was adept, too, with the long ball over the heads of full-backs, and delivered it as only a Brazilian seemed able to, with the ball checking its pace as it bounced.

Didi, who scored his goals with accuracy rather than venom, had a good World Cup,

Didi's pace might have been going. He had had eight rather exacting years at the top. But the brain was as sharp as ever. He knew too much for some rather undistinguished opposition and Brazil's veterans from the 1958 tournament were still the Champions.

Didi, who scored 24 goals in his 72 games for Brazil, finished his playing career in Peru before becoming that country's manager. He took Peru to the World Cup quarter-finals in Mexico, and just to prove that football talks its own universal language he later went and coached the Arabs in Saudi Arabia. It was not a coincidence that his team in Jeddah quickly won a reputation for being the most elegant side in Saudi Arabia.

Alfredo di Stefano

Argentina, Spain, River Plate,
Los Millionarios, Real Madrid, Espanol

Di Stefano was as complete a footballer as there can ever have been, especially as he played most of his career with his back to his

Di Stefano (right) scores one of his four goals in the European Cup Final of 1960—a match still talked of by those who were at Hampden Park to see it.

Didi, Brazil's midfield star of 1958, when managing Peru in the 1970 World Cup finals.

but really reached his peak in Sweden in 1958 when he had Garrincha and Zagalo down the touchlines and, subsequently, the young Pelé to nurse through the competition.

It was the brilliance of Didi which influenced Brazil to start using the 4-2-4 system, and with four strikers to feed off, Brazil turned on fine exhibitions of attacking football in match after match.

Everybody was impressed, particularly the Spaniards. Real Madrid dangled the cash and Didi came to Europe. The move cost him his place in the Brazil side, but he was back for the World Cup in Chile.

opponents. He wore the No. 9 shirt, but was so much more than just a striker.

Perhaps he might be described as the first of the target men, but he had all the skills of a midfield player of world class to throw in as a bonus.

Until di Stefano, all centre-forwards had been purely goalscorers, but di Stefano, the highest-paid player in the world in his great days with Real when they made the European Cup almost their personal property, added a new dimension.

He was able to take part in any passing movement no matter how quickly the ball was moved around, but the goals never stopped thundering in.

Di Stefano was European Footballer of the Year in 1957 and 1959. He won five European Cup winner's medals and seven Spanish League championship medals and was five times leading scorer in the Spanish League.

Born in Buenos Aires, he had won seven Argentinian caps when he crossed the Atlantic for the big money. The partnership he subsequently struck up with former Hungarian captain Ferenc Puskas for Real Madrid became one of soccer's great legends.

If the name of Alfredo di Stefano was on everyone's lips during the 1950s and 1960s,

his words were certainly not. While a top player, 'Stef' remained silent and aloof. When he did give an interview, he came over as an abrupt man, almost rude, and it was not until he went into management in the late 1960s that he altered his public image.

Despite this lack of lovability, di Stefano retained a massive fan following throughout his career. He was an idol, but the crowds worshipped him, necessarily, from afar. They were simply not allowed to identify with the man.

He was born in 1926, and was coached almost from the cradle by his soccer-loving father, a bus driver in the Argentinian capital.

Stef's mother wanted him to follow the family tradition and go into farming. But with the backing of his father, Alfredo stuck to football. At the age of 17, he became an amateur with the famous River Plate club, and after a year on loan at Huracan, he returned to Plate as a professional and was swiftly drafted into the first team.

His three seasons there produced a Championship medal and seven Argentinian caps. Patriots naturally trusted that this new and masterful centre-forward would stay in the national side for years to come. They had

Di Stefano leads out a Rest of the World side to play England in the FA Centenary match of 1963.

rather a nasty shock coming to them.

In 1949, di Stefano accepted a move to Colombia and signed for the ambitious Los Millionarios club. It caused uproar in the Argentine, but 'Stef', with his income multiplied many times over, had no reason to worry.

The Bogota scene held him for another three seasons. Long enough for Los Millionarios to win the League Championship twice. Then he was on the move again, this time to Real Madrid.

Another row followed, with Barcelona protesting that they had been first in the queue. Real kept him, however, and quickly discovered they had gained an absolute treasure.

Di Stefano also applied for Spanish nationality and went on to score 23 goals in 31 appearances for his adopted country.

At Real, stars came and stars went, but the king went on forever. His popularity scarcely wavered, and when he spearheaded an attack that comprised Rial, Gento, Kopa and Puskas, Real seemed almost unbeatable.

Perhaps Stef's finest night was the European Cup Final of 1960. Real hammered Eintracht Frankfurt 7-3 in an astonishing match at Hampden Park. Stef scored four of the seven, Ferenc Puskas – his great friend – the other three.

His last move, in 1964, was to Espanol. But the great days were over, the move never really took off, and the balding giant went into management, successfully guiding Boca Juniors in his native South America before finding new triumphs with Valencia back in Spain.

Peter Doherty

Northern Ireland, Coleraine, Glentoran, Blackpool, Manchester City, Derby County, Huddersfield Town, Doncaster Rovers

Peter Doherty's great career started, in

62

terms of the Football League, at Blackpool in 1933. It finished at Doncaster 20 years later and in between times he never stopped running.

He was, without any argument, the best, and sometimes the most controversial, inside-forward Northern Ireland ever produced.

Peter, red of hair and fiery of temperament, was three players rolled into one. He was a defender, an attacker and, best of all, a midfield man with unbelievable stamina. Colin Bell, of Manchester City and England, is the only modern British player who remotely compares with him.

Perhaps the greatest of the gifts that Peter bestowed upon the game was his own infectious enthusiasm. As a player he could win a game out of his own commitment. Later, as a manager, he will be forever associated with Northern Ireland's heady journey to the quarter-finals of the World Cup in Sweden in 1958.

Sixteen Irish caps seems almost an insulting reward for a player of his stature, until you remember the war years and the fact that his country then rarely played more than three matches a season.

There was a sharp scorn for the soccer system inbred in Doherty. It placed him years ahead of most of his contemporaries who were simply glad to get themselves out of the dole queue. Peter, I am told, always wanted something better.

His abrasive nature led, inevitably, to clashes with the authorities. It also led, more sadly still, to his premature disenchantment with the game.

Peter was born in Coleraine, the Irish town whose soccer side gave him his first, unexpected break at the age of 15.

The story goes that Coleraine invited him for a trial one Saturday. When Doherty got to the ground, officials were panicking because the first-team right-winger had failed to turn up for the day's Irish League match.

Peter was hurried into shirts and shorts

The complete inside forward, Peter Doherty, the best Northern Ireland have had.

and sent out to deputise. Nobody passed to him, nobody talked to him, and when the missing winger arrived after half-time, young Doherty was instantly withdrawn and forgotten.

It was a year later when he was again recommended to Coleraine – by a sweet-shop owner if you please – and given another trial. This time, he was a greater success.

His next club was Glentoran, and then he moved to Blackpool in 1933. It was there, in England for the first time, that his speed, stamina and goalscoring ability made a striking impression. Within a year, he was in the Ireland side at inside-left.

Manchester City bought him in 1936 and won the Championship the following year. Doherty's contribution was to score 30 goals in 41 League games. A star was now, very clearly, born.

In the following two seasons, he added

63

another 40 League goals, averaging almost one every other game. Wartime then made the cut in his career. He joined the RAF but was, through being based at Loughborough, able to go on playing soccer in the war games for Derby County.

The link he forged with Raich Carter during these years was swiftly and surprisingly reformed when League football returned. Carter was sold by Sunderland, City agreed to let Doherty go, and Derby bought them both.

The first FA Cup Final after the war saw Derby beat Charlton 4-1. But it needed extra-time to separate the teams, thanks to a Charlton equaliser which deflected tragically off Doherty. He atoned with the crucial first goal in the extra period – at the right end.

Doherty's spell with Derby was an overnight triumph. And it met a swift end. He quarrelled with his bosses and was sold to Huddersfield.

By 1949, he was making his tentative entry into management, with Doncaster Rovers. As player-manager, he guided them up to the Second Division, and was still scoring goals when he retired in 1953.

There were times in the 1950s when, as manager of Bristol City and Northern Ireland, Doherty looked likely to become as big a success in that section of the game as he had been as a player. He was restless, though, and fierily ambitious. Eventually, he opted out.

Dragan Dzajic

Yugoslavia, Red Star Belgrade

Surely one of the most exciting players produced by Yugoslavia, Dzajic was capped more than 80 times.

He made a big impact on the European Nations' Cup tournament of 1968 when his goal knocked out England in the semi-final in Florence.

Dragan Dzajic was denied a victors' medal because after a 1-1 draw, the Yugoslavs were beaten 2-0 by Italy in the replay, but by then his name was a household word among neutral observers. Not surprisingly he was voted Footballer of the Year in his own land for three successive years, from 1968 to 1970.

He was the type of winger whom any manager would be glad to sign and, indeed, he received many offers to play in Western Europe. Speed, skill and a powerful shot were credentials that made him a feared adversary on good and bad pitches. He possessed wonderful close ball control and developed an ability to take on full-backs off either foot, a technique which severely added to their problems whenever he ran at them.

Red Star were a powerful force during much of his service with them and in 1968 they won both the League Championship and the Cup.

That year of 1968 was the making of Dzajic. English players, not surprisingly, christened him 'Magic Dragan' because of his astonishing ability to dribble. Right or left, it mattered little which side the defenders were. And he was an automatic choice for the Rest of the World team which played Brazil in the winter of 1968.

Traditionally he was an outside-left. But he loved to wander into the middle of the field in the same manner as Italy's Riva, and thunder goals in. If anything he had the edge on the Italian. Where Riva was heavy, Dzajic was a ballet dancer of a player and more of an irritant to opposing defenders by the exquisite and detached way in which he beat them.

Even when Dzajic was playing badly, and that was not often, he would win matches with one touch, one burst. The game might be quiet, then Dzajic could take your breath away with one searing run.

On the field, Dzajic was big, very big. Off the field he was a modest man, a schoolteacher.

Dragan Dzajic of Yugoslavia streaks away from his marker.

Dzajic being challenged by Pereira of Brazil in the 1974 World Cup finals.

Duncan Edwards

England, Manchester United

Duncan Edwards lost his life after the Munich air disaster. He was but a few months beyond his 21st birthday and was going to become just about the best footballer England had ever produced.

That was the opinion of most of us in the months before his death.

Duncan was born in the Black Country in Dudley. Perhaps he should have gone to his local club, Wolves. But that instinct, which was to win many a match, took him to Old Trafford where Matt Busby was running his academy for Soccer babes.

It was a decision that marked him as wise beyond his years. So did his football. For all his huge size, he could play touch football with the best of them. But if the touch was delicate then the tackle certainly was not.

Duncan was wearing his pyjamas when he signed for Manchester United. It was the early hours of the first day of October, 1952 – Duncan's 16th birthday – and United coach Bert Whalley had won the race to be first to a boy who had already caused a considerable stir at schoolboy level.

Duncan had grown up in Dudley, and when he was 11, played regularly in the town schoolboy team of 15-year-olds. That was symptomatic of the rest of his short life, for, as Sir Matt Busby once said: 'Duncan was never really a boy. In football terms, he was a man when he came to Old Trafford at 16.'

When he joined United, he was already

This stained glass window in his church at Dudley commemorates the life of Duncan Edwards.

God is with us for our Captain.

WRENS NEST BOWLING CLUB

Thanking God for the Life of Duncan Edwards, died at Munich, February 1958.

This picture of the 19-year-old Duncan Edwards gives some idea of his imposing physique, 13 stone, nearly six feet tall, and with thighs which resembled tree trunks.

13 stone and almost six feet tall; the possessor of a juddering tackle that can be compared only to Dave Mackay's in recent times.

Edwards made his League debut for United only six months after joining them and had played for England at every level by the time he was 18.

He played in England's first-ever Under-23 international and was then picked for the full national team, against Scotland, in April of 1955. This honour made him England's youngest-ever international, and to complete the occasion, Scotland were vanquished 7-2.

Over the next 34 months, Duncan was to play in 18 internationals. By the time he died, the nation had accepted him without question as their next captain; the man to lead them into World Cup combat for probably the next ten years.

Edwards was never an especially voluble man. Strong and silent sums him up as well as anything. His life was devoted to football, which in turn seemed to have devoted itself to bestowing as many talents on Duncan as on any other player in history.

Much has been said and written about the legend of Edwards, but perhaps nothing more significant than the comments of his United and England teammate Bobby Charlton: 'When I think of Duncan, I feel the rest of us were like pygmies. He was terrific. A professional through and through.'

Duncan had the quality of versatility on his side; he could, and frequently did, switch from his regular left-half position to play at centre-half, centre-forward or inside-left. Many assumed that he would make the England No. 5 shirt his own for the duration of the 1960s.

He was also enormously strong, enabling him to play 94 matches during the 1956-57 season. His tackling could be fierce, but never dirty.

When one thinks of the Busby Babes, Duncan Edwards is the first name which springs to mind. His influence, more than any other, drove them to the League Championship in 1956 and again the following year, when they might easily have become the first double-winners of the twentieth century but for an injury to goalkeeper Ray Wood during the FA Cup final.

Edwards played a total of only 151 League games for United—a short career in which to base the legend that undoubtedly still surrounds his name today.

On February 5, 1958, in faraway Belgrade, he played the last competitive football match of his life. It is bitterly ironic that he had never hidden his intense dislike of flying. The Munich air disaster claimed his life only after 15 days of fighting for survival in a hospital. It is said that his dying words included a question to Jimmy Murphy, Matt Busby's assistant: 'What time is the kick-off against Wolves, Jimmy? I can't afford to miss that one.'

Eusebio

Portugal, Lourenço Marques Sporting Club, Benfica

They called Eusebio the 'Black Panther'. They also called him the 'European Pelé'. Extravagant maybe, because Pelé was still thrilling the world when Eusebio had been forced to vacate the stage.

Eusebio was an exceptional player, nevertheless, and one of the best strikers of a ball the game has ever produced. Eusebio meant goals, dramatic goals. Which is possibly a pity, because the deserved reputation the boy from Mozambique had for goals of great power and beauty tended to mask the effect of his midfield work.

No way was Eusebio ever just a hitter of goals. Through the middle 1960s he kept Benfica among Europe's foremost clubs and Portugal, hitherto no menace to anybody, among the most successful national sides.

He was at his most dominating during the 1966 World Cup in England when single-handed he took Portugal into the semi-finals and a confrontation with his arch-rival Nobby Stiles. He was European Foot-baller of the Year in 1965, won a European Cup medal with Benfica in 1962 and runners-up medals on three other occasions.

Eusebio, first and foremost, was a tremendous athlete. He was not tall, but he had extremely wide shoulders and hefty thighs that pumped him over the ground at remarkable speed. At his best he must have seemed like a blur to opposition defenders. They saw him coming and then he was gone, past them before the tackle was possible.

And how he could shoot. Cannon-ball shots, swerving shots, shots from the sharpest of angles, he had them all. He also had remarkable nerve from the penalty spot, and yet there was always the suspicion that

The Black Panther pounces. Eusebio playing for Portugal against Hungary in the 1966 World Cup Finals in England.

when the going got really tough Eusebio lost some of his keenness.

Certainly he could not take stick and then come back in the same way that George Best could. Eusebio always gave the impression that the crowds wanted to see him play and should be given the opportunity of doing so.

Players like Nobby Stiles of Manchester United and England, did not see it quite that way, though Stiles was nothing like as hard on Eusebio as a lot of Continental defenders.

English fans had the good fortune to see a lot of Eusebio during the 1960s and they saw him at his best when he gave one of the finest individual performances of all time to keep Portugal in the World Cup of 1966.

Portugal were playing against the tiny North Koreans in the quarter-final. The Asians had already knocked-out Italy and it was odds on Portugal being the next ignominious victims when, incredibly, they were 3-0 down soon after the start.

The world waited for another soccer earthquake. Eusebio did not. Bang, bang, bang, bang. Portugal were leading 4-3. And Eusebio had got the lot, one explosion after another.

He also won a cheque for £1,000 for scoring most goals, nine, in the World Cup finals.

The lad who was born and grew up in a shack in the poorer quarter of Lourenço Marques, capital of Portuguese East Africa, had come a long way.

Eusebio was born into poverty in January, 1942. He was one of eight children whose father died when he was only five. At school he was an all-round sportsman, doubling basketball flair with the ability to beat most in a sprint. He signed for Lourenço Marques Sporting Club, became a professional when he was 17, and kicked-off with a hat-trick against famed Juventus.

It could not be long before Portugal called.

Eusebio (red shirt) playing against Bulgaria in the 1966 World Cup.

Benfica wanted him, and so did Sporting Club of Lisbon. The wrangle went on for months, but eventually Benfica got their man.

The immediate impact was hardly short of sensational. After only 25 matches he was in the Portugal team and played his second international at Wembley in 1961 when he was 19. He foretold the future well by thundering two shots against the cross-bar.

Eusebio had arrived. He stayed long enough to upstage Pelé by scoring a hat-trick in ten minutes when Pelé's Santos played Benfica . . . long enough to upstage di Stefano, Puskas, Santamaria and Gento when scoring twice in Benfica's 5-3 European Cup final win over Real Madrid . . . long enough after 1966 and the 1968 European Cup final which Manchester United won at Wembley, to become one of the most popular of players.

Though, commercially, he knew what his worth was, he made surprisingly few enemies.

Eventually his sharpness had to be replaced by stamina. He had to make way for the new generation at Benfica, but he could not give the game up. As late as 1978 he was still playing in the Portuguese Second Division.

Giacinto Facchetti

Italy, Inter-Milan

Facchetti is one of football's phenomena. For years the world has been waiting for the popular Italian captain to retire. And yet he goes on, and on, and on.

In the summer of 1978 he was preparing to play in his fourth World Cup, and looking hardly an ounce heavier than when he came into the Inter-Milan team in the early 1960s.

It is difficult to pinpoint any one aspect of Facchetti that makes him so exceptional until you are reminded that he has been through the complete transition and re-birth of the Italian national team and survived.

His main quality then, could be largely

inspirational. At the same time there can hardly have been a full-back of genuine world class who has scored so many goals as he. That's not necessarily because he has been playing a long time.

Facchetti was scheduled to go to Argentina at the ripe old age of 36. Twelve years earlier he had been in England when Italy had one of their most monumental playing disasters. They were knocked out of the World Cup by North Korea and returned home to anything but a hero's welcome. Most of the shame-faced players slunk back, but Facchetti was excused from the general abuse.

That is interesting because Facchetti was hardly a youngster on whom the disappointed Italians could take pity. He was a fully-fledged international.

He had played a key part in Inter's catenaccio-style defence when his club had won the European Cup in 1964 when they defeated Real Madrid 3-1 and followed this by winning it again with a narrow victory over Benfica in 1965. In 1965 they also won the World Club championship. And Italy had planned part of their 1966 World Cup strategy on Milan's success.

The only inference is that tall, spindly Facchetti, whose build looked suited to anything but full-back play had become a folk hero at an early age.

Come 1968, Facchetti was captain of Italy, an Italian team gradually throwing more emphasis on attack. They were trying to put adventure into their play but were still liable to revert to type, a dull, boring style, with the traditional amount of physical contact.

Perhaps this is where Facchetti scored, metaphorically. He did not go round kicking people. He strolled, seemingly aloof, and with all the time in the world to get where the ball was and haul Italy out of trouble.

Giacinto Facchetti, a stalwart of Inter-Milan throughout nearly two decades and four times in Italy's World Cup finals squad.

The Italian fans might easily have seen in him the prototype for what they wanted all their players to be.

In 1968, Facchetti captained Italy to victory in the European Nations Cup and he stayed as his country's leader for another ten years, a tremendous achievement in these days of high competition.

He led Italy to the final of the 1970 World Cup when Brazil beat them 4-1 in Mexico City. And was there again in West Germany in 1974 when Italy surprisingly failed to make the quarter-finals.

By 1971 he had become Italy's most capped player when he made his 61st appearance. Yet seven years later he was still in the side, aiming to set up unbeatable records.

To watch Facchetti play in the late 1970s is to wonder. By now a veteran, he should have trouble in turning and more trouble staying with players when the ball comes into defensive areas. It is a tribute to a fine football brain that he manages to avoid being turned inside out.

He has always been superb in the air which is not a bad attribute against teams like England and Scotland. Somebody has to show courage and get in there among them.

Facchetti's bravery has never been in question, probably a throw-back to his original days when he was a goalscoring centre-forward.

Fortunately for Inter and Italy, he has never lost that thirst for goals, and was probably the first of the successful over-lapping full-backs. If that is a claim to be disputed, then certainly he must rank as the most durable.

Though he plays the game in a gentlemanly fashion, forwards have learned that he is not the player nor the man with whom to take liberties. He can be tough and un-compromising as well as a fine tactician.

He joined Inter at the age of 18 and won his first cap in March, 1963. He seems certain to become a manager of some repute.

Tom Finney

England, Preston North End

Tom Finney was the complete player. He had everything, including loyalty. He had marvellous natural ability and was so two-footed that I would not like to say which was his most effective foot, either for shooting, crossing or dribbling.

His loyalty to his home town club he demonstrated by refusing an offer to go to Italy for huge money at a time in the early 1950s when English players were earning not much more than an average working man's wage.

He spent most of his time at Preston making life unpleasant for left-backs. Towards the end he was doing the same for centre-halves. Body swerves and feints made him very special. He could beat any opponent, he could pass under pressure and he had a devastating shot. When I was a young player with Brentford we faced Preston and Finney on a mud-heap. There was grass down the touchline and up along the goal-line. While we ploughed through the mud, Finney used the grass. We lost 4-2, and Finney made all their goals.

Fans might have preferred Stan Matthews in the great controversy over who was the better player. Managers would have preferred Finney.

Johnny Haynes, playing as usual at inside left, once got three goals for England. It might have had something to do with Finney at centre-forward.

It was no accident that Tom spent his career with Preston, for he also spent his formative Saturday afternoons there, standing with his father and learning to idolise Alex James.

Finney was only seven years old when James left Deepdale for Highbury. It broke Tom's heart but failed to turn him against his home club.

He tried to copy James' skills on the pavements near his house, and at 15, he went to Deepdale for coaching sessions. He

Facchetti, wearing the captain's armband, defending as calmly as ever against Brazil.

was 4ft 9in tall and weighed five stone!

At this stage, he favoured the left-wing position and insisted on wearing the baggy shorts made famous by James. In his first official trial for the club, however, he was switched to the right side, where he was to make himself famous.

An oddity in Finney's early career is the fact that he turned down a job as a ground-staff boy—always considered the spring-board to the playing staff—in favour of learning a trade. As it turned out, he was just being sensible, and the plumbing proficiency he cultivated established him in a profitable business in later years.

Tom Finney was only 17 when war broke out, and he could ignore it no better than any other footballer. He starred in Preston's defeat of Arsenal in the 1941 War Cup final, then left the game to serve in the Army.

Naturally enough, it was 1946 before he was able to resume playing . . . 1946 before he was able to even make his debut in the Football League. That day came in August, and one month later, Finney pulled on an England shirt for the first time.

His early international opportunity came only because the maestro, Stan Matthews, was injured. But when, two months later, Matthews was fit and available, England overlooked him and retained Finney for a match against Wales. It was a move that caused a great split among soccer followers, the fans of Matthews and Finney indulging in heated debates which ignored the fact that the two men were close friends—and remained so.

It was undoubtedly a sticky one for the selectors, though, and they finally solved it by switching Finney to outside-left. He professed a dislike for the position, but retained it for 33 of his 76 internationals—and played a further three at centre-forward.

Some of his greatest games were played at

Tom Finney in 1956 wearing the shirt of
Preston North End, his only club.

Hampden Park. The Scots grew to hate him,
for in six internationals he played on that
ground, England never lost once.

At club level, he was part of a Preston side
which promised a great deal, but ultimately
achieved nothing. They were League
runners-up to Arsenal in 1953, and the
following season they reached Wembley.
The Cup final was against West Bromwich
Albion and the uncommitted thought, and
probably hoped, that this would be Finney's
day. Instead, it was one of his most dis-
appointing displays and Preston were beaten
3-2.

In all, he played 431 League games for
Preston, appearing in each of the five forward positions. And, to the people of the
town, he became a king. When he retired at
the age of 38, 30,000 fans turned up to
watch his farewell game – a meaningless
affair against Luton Town. The following
year, Preston were relegated, and the locals
said they knew the reason why.

Just Fontaine

France, Nice, Rheims

No one contributed more to France's
magnificent performances in the 1958 World
Cup finals in Sweden than Just Fontaine,
that sturdy attacker with the fierce shot.

His sense of position, perception and
ability to punish defensive errors brought
him 13 goals in that series which is a World
Cup record.

He scored three times in France's 7-3
rout of the Paraguayans in the group
matches and when he netted against Brazil
in the semi-finals, it was the first goal the
South American champions had conceded
in the tournament. Sadly for Fontaine there

**Thirteen goals in the 1958 World Cup
finals is the proud record held by France's
Just Fontaine, later France's manager.**

was no happy ending because the Brazilians took control in the second half, with a 17-year-old called Pelé showing glimpses of the natural gifts which were to make him a world soccer figure. In the end France were comprehensively destroyed to the tune of five goals to two, but long before then Fontaine had captured the imagination of the writers and public alike. They enthused over his all-round talents and those of his colleagues, Raymond Kopa and Roger

Hughie Gallacher is often called 'the greatest centre-forward of all time'.

Piantoni. They were an exciting triumvirate and I doubt very much whether French football has ever witnessed a finer combination than these three 'Musketeers'.

Fontaine's club, Rheims, were an influential force in their country's league and cup programmes during the 1950s and early 1960s, twice winning the domestic championship and the Cup. They were also Real Madrid's opponents in the first European Champions' Cup Final of 1956 and again in 1959. Both games were lost to the Spaniards but Fontaine, who played in the 1958-59 series, finished leading scorer with 10 goals.

Fontaine was born in Marrakesh, Morocco and Nice introduced him into League football. He soon caught the eye of those responsible for choosing the national side and in October, 1956, he was given his chance at centre-forward against the Hungarians at Colombes, but France were defeated 2-1 and Fontaine went back to the drawing board for a year.

By the time he went to the World Cup finals at Sweden, Fontaine had proved his worth at inside-forward. Yet he did not anticipate winning a place in the team. Only when Bliard was hurt was Fontaine brought into action—with remarkable results. In addition to the three he scored against Uruguay, he demoralised the West German defence in the third place play-off game and helped himself to four goals in France's 6-3 success.

Unhappily a fractured leg brought Fontaine's career as a striker to a premature end but nothing can detract from his service to French soccer. In later years he managed the national squad for a while.

Hughie Gallacher

Scotland, Queen of the South, Airdrie, Newcastle United, Chelsea, Derby, Notts County, Grimsby, Gateshead

In the 1920s and 1930s centre-forwards were supposed to be big men. It was tough in the opposing penalty box and there was no way a tiny fellow of 5ft 5in could survive. But there was one exception, Hughie Gallacher, a fierce competitive Scot with a hard, mining village background.

It follows that he had to be quite a bit of a footballer, too, and this Gallacher certainly was. He played his first Scottish League matches for Airdrie in 1921-22 and when he played his last first-class matches with Gateshead in 1938-39 he was still good enough to get 18 goals in 31 matches, at the age of 36.

Gallacher was more than just a footballer. On the field he was a genius. Off the field he was, to put it mildly, an amazing character.

He was also a chip-on-the-shoulder star, complaining bitterly to officialdom that referees never gave him the protection to which he was entitled.

There has never been a footballer with a life-style like Gallacher's. Gallacher was often dubbed 'the greatest centre-forward of all time'. He was the hero of thousands. Yet he endured more mental anguish off the

Gallacher playing for Chelsea in 1931 challenges the Leicester goalkeeper who has just punched the ball away.

field than any of his followers could ever have known.

It began when he defied the wishes of his parents and married a local Lanarkshire girl. He was just 17 and they stayed together only a year. Their son died before his first birthday and although the daughter they produced brought a brief reunion, they parted permanently when Hughie was 20.

Years later, Gallacher was charged with ill-treating the daughter, and on the eve of the court case, he committed suicide by throwing himself in front of an express train.

His death occurred in 1957 and he had been out of League soccer for 18 years. Many still treasured his memory – the memory of the days at Newcastle and Chelsea, and his starring role in the Scotland forward-line which fashioned the 5-1 destruction of England in 1928.

Oddly, Alex James played alongside Hughie in that famed international, just as he had done almost two decades earlier, when Gallacher and James were names on the teamsheet at a junior school in Bellshill.

Gallacher's love for football helped him through the First World War, when he worked in a munitions factory – and afterwards, when he followed local custom and took a mining job.

When he was 17, he scored a late winner for Scotland juniors against Ireland, and attracted immediate attention from Queen of the South. He signed, for £6 per week, but made little headway at the club due to an attack of double pneumonia.

While he was still recovering from the illness, Airdrie offered him half as much again as Queen of the South were paying, and he signed for a club who were, at the time, high in Scotland's First Division.

He averaged almost a goal a game at Airdrie, scoring 91 times in 111 League matches spread over five seasons. Inevitably, English clubs showed an interest, and in November 1925, Newcastle paid £6,500 for the small Scotsman.

He was made captain at Newcastle within a year. It was a departure from tradition, both to have such a young skipper and to have a centre-forward in the job. But he silenced any doubters by leading Newcastle to the League Championship in his first season as captain.

His goals in Geordieland frequently arrived in floods of three or four. Just as they were to love Malcolm Macdonald 50 years later, the north-eastern fanatics warmed to Hughie and treated him possessively. The town was stunned when he joined Chelsea for £10,000 in 1930.

It was around this time that Gallacher brushed with soccer authority. He was sent off and suspended for two months for dissent. The referee involved was called Fogg. When his suspension was over, Gallacher was instantly back in the Scotland side to play Ireland. Mr Fogg was, coincidentally, the man in charge – and Hughie scored five times!

Spells at Derby, Notts County, Grimsby and Gateshead followed his four seasons at Stamford Bridge. Gallacher totalled more than 500 League games – and scored 387 goals. In internationals, his striking rate was a remarkable 22 goals in 19 games for Scotland. His death was a tragic postscript to a magic career.

Garrincha

Brazil, Botafogo, Corinthians, Flamengo

If ever in the history of the World Cup there is an instance of one player winning a tournament, then it happened in Chile in 1962, and Garrincha, a right-winger with a unique style, was the man who did it.

On the record, Brazil simply retained the trophy they had won four years earlier in Sweden. But the record is an over simplification. Brazil were then an ageing team and they were without the injured Pelé for most of the finals. Without Garrincha's influence there must be a doubt whether Brazil would have succeeded.

Garrinchas are little birds that fly in the mountain village of Pau Grande, just outside Rio. Young Manoel Francisco dos Santos used to go out and shoot them. But once he came to the notice of the Rio soccer fanatics and the Botafogo club, nobody ever called him dos Santos again.

Little Bird was a one-off, and will stay that way until somebody finds another player with such exceptional ability and whose legs are of different lengths. Garrincha, astonishingly, was born a cripple and needed an operation to allow him to walk.

Yet he won two World Cup winner's medals and 68 caps with Brazil. Not bad after starting as an inside-forward and becoming an outside-right only because it was the only way he could play in a trial match at Botafogo. Having run rings round Nilton Santos, the national left-back who was also Botafogo's No. 3, Garrincha never went back to inside-forward.

But for Nilto, and Brazil's midfield star Didi, Garrincha might never have played in the 1958 World Cup. It was they, when Brazil were not functioning properly in Sweden, who went to the selection committee and demanded Garrincha's inclusion. They knew what they were talking about!

When British journalists first saw Garrincha they called him the Stanley Matthews of Brazil. But the only similarity was the No. 7 shirt they both wore. Garrincha had electric pace over longer than Stanley's first half-dozen yards. He also had a fair shot which Stanley might have had but declined so often to use.

Garrincha was also a very good header of a ball, and the number of times Stanley headed can almost be remembered. He could also bend a shot like no European, until then, thought possible.

Under pressure, he could still hit the target with a low pass to anybody hanging back in the middle. But without any doubt, his greatest asset was speed. He was almost impossible to tackle.

He caused defenders to hesitate in the tackle. They knew that if they missed he would be gone. There would be no hope of catching him. He looked fragile, but was strong. He could resist and ride tackles. Despite the operation he had the strength in his legs to stay upright when lesser players might have fallen.

Garrincha's biggest trouble, once he stopped playing football, was an innocence that owed its origin to his country upbringing. He never lost it. What he lost instead was a huge amount of money. Some of it went on raising a family of seven children. More of it went on an expensive divorce to a singer that made him virtually an outcast in Brazilian social society.

But that came later, after Garrincha had dominated Chile, choosing England in the quarter-finals as the side against which to give his best performance. It was not a bad England team, either.

The defence included Jimmy Armfield, Ray Wilson, Maurice Norman and the young Bobby Moore. Behind them was the goalkeeping experience of Ron Springett.

But Garrincha outjumped big Norman to head the first; produced the second after Springett had been forced to drop his free-kick at Vava's feet; and scored the third himself by bending the ball round Springett. England lost 3-1.

Garrincha went back to Rio in triumph. It was as well he enjoyed the adulation then because he was passing the peak of his career. He hurt a knee playing for Botafogo. Medical opinion was that he should rest for three months. Unfortunately, Botafogo had arranged a tour. Without Garrincha, the guarantees would be far less. Unwilling to lose the money, Botafogo forced the Little Bird to play. From then on, his wings were clipped.

He came to England for the 1966 World Cup, but was obviously not the same player.

Botafogo, and Brazil, had Jairzinho waiting in the wings. Goodison Park, where Garrincha scored one delightful goal by

Garrincha, Brazil's great right winger about to go round a German defender at the Maracana Stadium.

swerving a free-kick past the Bulgarians, was virtually the swansong.

Garrincha's lack of business sense meant that he had to go on playing football. He went through a string of smaller clubs and eventually on to Mexico and soccer oblivion. But in 1962 the world had been his.

Francisco Gento

Spain, Real Madrid

Nobody in Spain ever referred to Gento, the most popular of Spanish footballers, other than by his nickname 'Paco'. He was one of that country's best-loved players probably because he was the Spaniard who could star in the great Madrid team when it was composed of famous Argentinians, Brazilians, Uruguayans and Hungarians.

Real, European Cup winners from 1956 to 1960 and again a sixth time in 1966 when they were skippered by the legendary Gento himself, were without much doubt the finest club side of all time. And Gento was the left-wing star.

Di Stefano got the glory. Puskas got the goals. Big Santamaria was the pivot all opposition feared. But out on the left wing was 'Paco', the happy Spaniard who was never happier than when at a bull fight.

Gento spent 18 years with Real, the last seven of them as skipper, before retiring at the end of the 1970-71 season.

He was a pure, specialist, uncomplicated outside-left. Full-backs who tried to catch him might have been chasing greyhounds.

Like most natural wingers, the danger he created came not so much from his speed over the ground but from his quickness off the mark. He might have been designed to be a winger: average height, average weight, strong legs and a fine tactical brain.

He learned a lot from di Stefano, and was certainly not outclassed in that famous company, not even when he came in as a boy.

81

Gento, a Spaniard in Real Madrid's 'international' forward line, was the fastest left winger of modern times.

It was a simple game the way Gento played it, and how beautifully effective.

The ball would fly out to the wing from di Stefano, perfectly measured to catch Gento in mid-stride as he flew past the bemused back. Up to the goal-line, a perfect centre, and probably half the Real team were lined up to score.

I remember seeing him at Stamford Bridge in an Old Internationals match. It was about five years since he and George Cohen, England's right-back in the 1966 World Cup final, had stopped playing. George could move a bit, too, and the pair of them went down that touchline, neither giving an inch as the years rolled away.

At his peak, it was said of Gento that he could give any full-back five yards start in ten and beat him. Exaggeration, yes, but it paints the picture.

As his game matured Gento became a

fixture in the Spanish team, and he had won 44 caps when he called it a day, no doubt to concentrate on the bulls.

Gento so loved the sport that he used to go down into the ring and train with the matadors. It may have improved his footwork, but it did nothing for the Real officials' nerves. Several times they imposed heavy fines on Gento. But they could not stop him. Neither could many full-backs.

Johnny Giles

Ireland, Manchester United, Leeds United, West Bromwich Albion

Johnny Giles was a midfield artist of patience, guile and hidden aggression. The perfect cog in the centre of a team.

He had such a good sense of positional play that he was always there when needed and nearly always followed the gaining of possession by speeding the ball to precisely the right spot to be most effective.

He was a wonderful player for his colleagues, always there to get them out of trouble. Despite his small frame, it was almost impossible to dispossess him when he was in control of the ball. He was so nimble that he found extra agility and turning capacity. So much so that opponents who knew him well preferred to back off rather than risk what would almost certainly be a wasted tackle.

Giles was also one of those very gifted players who had a lovely feel for the ball. He could coax it on for two or three yards at just the right pace or hit a 50-yard through ball. His all-round vision of the play was so good he could spot people going at that distance and drop the pass to the inch.

Giles, one of the great soccer brains since he first got into the Manchester United team in 1959-60, was certainly no ordinary midfield player. He had a gift for goals as well. Many are the times he has scored when the

Giles playing on a muddy pitch against Arsenal at Highbury in 1975.

situation and the occasion have demanded a goal. He had a hard dig in those small feet as many a goalkeeper could testify after being beaten from just outside the penalty box. The reason he scored fewer than he might have done while masterminding Leeds' unprecedented sequence of success is simply that he was so valuable a part in the centre of the Leeds machine that they couldn't allow him to play much further up front.

Giles was a winger when he first went to Manchester from a junior club in his native Dublin. He won an FA Cup medal at Old Trafford in 1963 when United beat Leicester 3-1. But I think it was experience gained out there on the right touchline that gave Giles the confidence to hold the ball.

Too many of today's midfield men treat the ball as though it is a hot potato. They want to get rid of it before they have had a chance to set up an attack. Not Giles.

Giles was happy to hold the ball, and quite capable of holding it, until he could do the right thing with it. This factor accounted for much of his genius.

Perhaps, in retrospect, selling Giles might have been one of Sir Matt Busby's rare errors when he was managing Manchester United. But Giles, deep thinking and ambitious, was ready to go.

He always felt that playing on the wing never gave him the opportunity to run a game. There was always an orchestra leader waiting to burst from the fiddler on the right.

Leeds manager Don Revie got his man for £37,500, a ridiculously small fee. But Giles was still out on the right. Eventually, in 1965, Leeds midfield maestro Bobby Collins, the old Scotland star, was severely injured. He was going to be out of the game for a long time.

Giles moved inside and into the role for which he had been waiting. From then on until he left Elland Road, Giles was king.

The mastermind of Leeds United's great team of the 1960s and 1970s, Johnny Giles.

Other Leeds players might have grabbed bigger headlines. Giles was the player they most missed when he was injured.

Giles did most good by comparative stealth, and has an analytical brain he used just as effectively in other directions.

While he was at Leeds, always quietly in the background at any club social occasion, he secured his future by developing business interests outside the game. Inside the game, he continued at Elland Road until Revie departed to become manager of England.

The Leeds team would have to be broken up. Giles had been a successful player-manager of the Republic of Ireland team. When West Bromwich wanted him as their player-manager, the opportunity was too good to miss.

Giles, an individual, his own man to the core, stayed two years after wanting to leave after the first 12 months. They were successful seasons, but his independent spirit found directors too stultifying to live with.

He went, with no ill-feeling, back home to Dublin where he bought a part-share in Shamrock Rovers, became managing director and continued as part-time manager of the national team.

Giles had always been boss on the field. Off it, he could only live happily if he was boss there, too.

Billy Gillespie, scorer of both goals in a 2-1 victory for Northern Ireland over England on his first appearance in 1913.

Billy Gillespie

Northern Ireland, Leeds, Sheffield United

Northern Ireland has produced many exciting and creative forwards. One thinks quickly of Peter Doherty, George Best, Jimmy McIlroy and Billy Bingham to mention just a few of the gifted, attack-minded players who have donned the green jersey in recent years. In any list of this character you could never omit Billy Gillespie, a shrewd tactician who served both his country and Sheffield United so well before and after the First World War. Astonishingly, he made his final international appearance against England at Sheffield in October, 1930, 17 years after his debut as a centre-forward in Belfast in February, 1913. He marked that initial appearance by scoring both goals to give the Irish a memorable 2-1 victory, their first in 32 attempts dating back to the first meeting in 1882. One can only imagine the celebrations that went on in the Northern Ireland capital that night when Gillespie's name must have been on the lips of every Irish soccer enthusiast as they toasted their victorious countrymen in a 'drop of the hard stuff'.

Gillespie started his playing life with Leeds but after 24 games he joined Sheffield United and set out on a remarkable career of 20 years with the Bramall Lane club. There are still supporters of United who will tell you that 'Billy' was the finest of all forwards who have represented the club. And though I never had the opportunity of seeing him in action, I am certain from my own enquiries that there is much validity in their claim.

Because of premature baldness Gillespie was easily recognisable as he wove his skills and tormented opponents. He certainly showed a flair for scoring goals (including 13 for Northern Ireland) but his foremost talent lay in the way he fashioned openings for colleagues. He had that quality possessed by all the top flight scheming inside men of being able to turn defences inside out with one astutely timed pass or a sudden swerve of the body. One friend who remembers Gillespie in the late 1920s tells me that even at the end of his playing days he was still capable of making defenders leaden-footed and bereft of recovery by a single decisive thrust into the enemy's lines.

Undoubtedly one of the proudest moments in a crowded career occurred in 1925 when he captained Sheffield United to a 1-0 victory over Cardiff City in the FA Cup final at Wembley, the last time that the trophy has rested among the silverware at Bramall Lane.

He was also a member of the Northern Ireland team which won the International Championship outright for the only time to date, in 1913-14. In that season Ireland beat Wales 2-1 at Wrexham and England 3-0 at Middlesbrough (still their most clearcut success on English soil), and drew 1-1 with Scotland in Belfast.

Jimmy Greaves

England, Chelsea, AC Milan, Tottenham Hotspur, West Ham United

For most people, myself included, Jimmy Greaves was the greatest goalscorer in the history of the game. He had that indefinable something that when you saw it you said:

'That's Greaves'. And when you see the occasional flash of it from another player you say: 'Almost as good as Greaves'.

That Greaves is used as the yardstick is the finest tribute he can be paid.

His biggest asset was balance, even at speed. To change direction and keep going in the same movement is almost impossible. But Greaves could do it. He could drop a shoulder, jink, and be past opponents before they could see the trouble coming.

Why he took his goals so well was all a matter of temperament. He was so relaxed that I do not think he was any more excited at suddenly being in front of goal than he was cleaning his teeth in the morning.

The ability to beat goalkeepers in man-

against-man situations sums up Greaves. It is one of the hardest feats in the game because the angle always favours the goalkeeper. But a subtle placing, and the ball would be given just enough power to roll over the line. That was vintage Greaves.

Nobody else had his utter mastery of the last 20 yards of the field. Nobody blasted in so few goals. And nobody eased in so many with the defence in absolute disarray.

At 15 years of age, Greaves was earning a pittance as a teaboy with Chelsea. At 31, he lived with his wife and four children in a seven-bedroomed Essex house, worked as a partner in a highly profitable business, and confessed he had cut himself off entirely from the world of football.

The game lured him back to its lower reaches, but the comeback was distinctly forgettable. Greaves played for Chelmsford and then Barnet, both in the Southern League, but only succeeded in tarnishing his image by being sent off—and refusing to go—in a small-time midweek match. The man and his fans will not care to remember that night. I certainly do not wish to.

So we concentrate on the 16 years between 15 and 31. The golden years, when Greaves was incomparable, chased but never caught as the prince of poachers in front of goal.

Greaves playing for Spurs, about to be tackled by David Nish of Leicester.

The greatest goal-scorer in soccer, Jimmy Greaves slots one in for Chelsea against Everton.

His father was a London tube driver, and when he told son Jimmy to study a trade and put football second, he was saying nothing outrageous, merely voicing the economics of the 1950s, when even the top footballers were earning no more than £20 per week.

Jimmy was a determined lad, though, and we should all be grateful for that. An East London wartime baby, he was destined for stardom in West London from the moment that Chelsea won the scramble for his signature when he left school.

Between making his debut at the age of 17, oddly against Tottenham, and leaving Chelsea on an ill-fated move to Italy in 1960, Greaves played 169 first-team games and scored 132 goals.

His striking statistics alone are enough to frighten the most resilient defender. Greaves scored five goals in a match three times. Four in a match another three times. And nine hat-tricks, scored as if they were a habit.

He always insisted he enjoyed his football at Chelsea, but moved because he could see

it ended in a matter of months. Greaves came back to England. To Tottenham, who had beaten Chelsea to the punch and paid £99,999, the odd pound subtracted only because Bill Nicholson did not want him burdened with the first six-figure label.

It was hardly an easy time to join Spurs. They had, after all, just won the League and Cup double. Just how could Greaves fit in?

The question was answered with alacrity. Greaves scored three times on his debut against Blackpool, just to aptly usher in the greatest nine years of his career.

He was First Division top scorer three years in succession, totalled 220 League goals and helped Tottenham retain their berth at the top for several years.

He had his bad times, too. At the end of 1965, he suffered an attack of hepatitis. Although he would not admit it at the time, Greaves was never again as fast or sharp as he had been.

The critics also found something to snipe at. Despite his unrivalled goalscoring feats, they chose to lash him for a lack of effort, dedication and that modern catch-phrase 'work-rate'.

Jim himself names June 30, 1966, as the saddest day of his football life. It was the day on which England won the World Cup – and Jim sat on the subs' bench. He never played for England again, his 57 internationals and 44 goals being curtailed by a disagreement with Sir Alf Ramsey. Greaves was not prepared to attend Alf's training get-togethers if he was not due to play in the team. They agreed to differ.

The final days of the little man's career were played out at Upton Park, close to his birthplace. He joined them in March, 1970, valued at £54,000 in an exchange with Martin Peters.

But this was not the same Greaves – and by now, he knew it. On May 1, 1971, he played his last Football League match. Greaves, honest, humorous and as talented as any striker the world has seen, accepted it was time to go.

no possibility of winning anything. Greaves, fast becoming an English idol, chose the life of the European mercenary – and regretted it almost instantly.

Jim earned himself a fat signing-on fee and a healthy annual wage when he joined AC Milan. But he had scarcely left England when my lengthy fight for the abolition of the maximum wage was won. Jim had landed himself in a country he detested and in playing conditions he despised – all for the sort of money he could just as easily have picked up at home.

The Italian job was destined to failure and

Jimmy Hagan

England, Derby County, Sheffield United

Jimmy Hagan achieved considerable distinction both as a player and coach, yet for all his artistry as an inside-forward he won only one official cap. The truth, of course, was that like so many others of his vintage, Jimmy was possibly at the height of his power during the war years. He did, in fact, make as many as 17 appearances in wartime and 'Victory' internationals, but none of these counted so far as the award of caps was concerned.

In one of these wartime internationals he made a little niche for himself in the record books by scoring after only 50 seconds. That was against Scotland at Wembley in 1942.

His single official appearance for England came in a somewhat undistinguished team performance during September, 1948, when an unrated Denmark side held their visitors to a goalless draw in Copenhagen. England's forward line that day read: Stanley Matthews, Hagan, Tommy Lawton, Len Shackleton, and Bobby Langton, a star-studded enough line-up but, obviously, the combined genius of that particular quintet was muted by a superbly resolute Danish defence. Stan Mortensen was back as Matthews' partner for the next match and though Hagan's name was often put forward for further recognition, sadly it never again appeared in an England attack.

Jimmy played for Derby County from season 1935-36 until Sheffield United signed him in 1938. The wisdom of the move was quickly demonstrated when his inspirational play helped United to win promotion from the Second Division at the end of that season. They had missed going up the previous season only on goal average and this time they were involved in a desperate three-club challenge for the two places. Finally Blackburn took the title with 55

A thoughtful inside-forward, Jimmy Hagan became a much respected coach.

points, Sheffield United finished second with 54 and just a point further away were their neighbours, Sheffield Wednesday.

Jimmy always thought deeply about the game, so that it came as no surprise to his many friends when he turned to coaching on his retirement as a player. His facility for communication however, seemed to be more appreciated on the Continent than in England and for a time he managed the top Portuguese side, Benfica. He also had spells as manager at Peterborough and West Bromwich.

Eddie Hapgood

England, Arsenal

Until Billy Wright came to dominate the scene for so long, the appearances record for England was in the hands, or the elegant feet, of Eddie Hapgood, left-back of Arsenal and England for 12 full seasons until September, 1939.

In that time, Hapgood was the inspiration

Captain of Arsenal and England, Eddie Hapgood was renowned for anticipation and goal line clearances.

of both, a model player with unbounding enthusiasm who thought simply that Arsenal were the finest club in football and everybody should be proud to play for them.

During Hapgood's time at Highbury, Arsenal won the First Division championship five times and the FA Cup twice. Hapgood, cool, skilful, played more pure football from the rear of the team than many an orthodox inside-forward.

Until Hapgood, the brief for most full-backs was to heave the ball over the half-back line as soon as possible and as powerfully as possible. Overlapping was a tactic of the future, but football owes Hapgood a debt for demonstrating that good football can be played from a team's own goal-line.

Perhaps it was a measure of Arsenal's stature in those days that Hapgood had led England many times before being given the captaincy of Arsenal. For that, he had to wait until the great Alex James, ignored outrageously by Scotland, retired.

From meeting the dawn as a milkman to meeting royalty at a Wembley Cup Final was but a short step for Eddie Hapgood. Short, though, only due to the vigilance of Arsenal manager Herbert Chapman, who prised him away from non-League club Kettering when he had played scarcely more than a dozen games for them.

Hapgood had not been a footballer at school; in fact he had not seriously taken up the game until he started work, driving a horse-drawn milk cart in Bristol for his brother's firm.

Bristol Rovers had given him a trial and even offered terms. Eddie turned them down because, I understand, they wanted him to work the off-season periods on a coal cart. He stayed with milk and turned to non-League soccer.

Chapman came personally to Kettering and was quickly convinced that Hapgood was his man. Eddie's first journey to London was a disaster, however, for card-playing con-merchants stripped him of his £10 signing-on fee!

He made his debut for Arsenal in the 1927-28 season, just as the Gunners' glory days were being conceived. Within two seasons he was in the Cup-winning side at Wembley, and honours followed almost annually through the years up to the outbreak of war.

George Male joined Hapgood in the Arsenal side early in the 1930s – the birth of one of the finest full-back partnerships the game has seen. George and Eddie were to play together for Arsenal and England until the war and, in unofficial games, during the war.

As with most classic combinations, they were different in most ways, technically and temperamentally. The contrast was a huge success.

Hapgood was belligerent yet elegant. An ideal leader, it seemed. England, indeed, recognised his captaincy qualities first, and he led his country against Italy in 1934, only a year after winning his first cap – against the same opposition.

In all, he played 30 official internationals and 13 during the war. Of the total of 43, he was captain 34 times.

Eddie never played another League game after the war, although his retirement was not pre-decided. His relationship with Arsenal's new boss George Allison did not approach the professional intimacy he shared with Chapman, and in 1945 he retired, going on to managerial positions with Blackburn, Watford and Bath City before fading from the game completely.

Johnny Haynes

England, Fulham

Johnny Haynes was the master of any pass and a more prolific and accurate passer of a through ball than any other player I have seen.

He could run no faster than the average footballer, which in some respects was a handicap for an international forward. On the other hand he made up for this lack of extreme pace by incredible agility and quickness off the mark over short distances to either collect a ball or burst into space.

Johnny had another extraordinary asset. When he had to get to a ball he found an extra yard of pace from somewhere.

His control of the ball was immaculate, and he was a completely two-footed player. He could drop a 45-yard pass from the old inside-left position equally well with his left or his right foot.

It never surprises me that the most enthusiastic tributes to him come from those who had tried to mark him out of a game. This was almost impossible to accomplish because John had the capacity to screen a ball, using his more than amply-muscled backside to emphatic effect even against the strongest tacklers.

Tight marking can reduce players of outstanding skill, but nobody could be sure of doing that to Johnny when he had made up his mind to play.

The time would eventually come when the tackles would get too violent, but he would seldom turn a hair or think of retaliating. He was too busy trying to get on with the game.

Haynes, never the greatest individualist, firmly believed that the easiest way through a defence was by clever interpassing between groups of players. As he saw it, the problem was most simply solved by the ball and the player to go through separately and join at the perfect moment for the killer blow.

Johnny started his international career with players such as Matthews and Finney who both preferred the ball to their feet. Occasionally, it caused some friction. Matthews certainly did not take kindly to the young upstart telling him where he should run, but I can remember one match at Wembley against the Brazilians, who were using tight-marking full-backs, when Matthews made his through run and Haynes made his point by putting him straight through the defence in one move with a superbly placed ball.

The first English £100 per week footballer – Johnny Haynes.

It is not possible to strike the devastating sort of passes that Haynes was seeking without a fair percentage of errors, a circumstance that gave those who did not always appreciate the Haynes genius their chance to criticise.

It took a lot of courage for Haynes to continue to go for the difficult ball rather than the bread and butter safety pass, but Haynes had courage enough to spare in this respect.

Johnny seemed to have eyes in the back of his head, in that he had the capacity to spot his team-mates' movements almost as if there were some kind of extra-sensory perception. How he did it and managed to control a ball at the same time only Haynes or his instinct will ever know.

Though his figures faded in later years,

Johnny Haynes in typical attitude – controlling the ball in midfield before starting an attack for Fulham against Coventry in 1968.

Johnny was quite a goalscorer. It is a myth that he only made them. Yet it was in the business of shooting that I always felt he could have become a better player.

In season 1958-59 he scored no fewer than 26 in 34 League matches. There was a good reason. At the time he was being compared as a goal scorer with Bobby Charlton, who could then have been a rival rather than a colleague in the England side. Johnny

decided to score more goals, just to make his point.

He had the ability to strike the ball at goal with enough power in either foot, but frequently when in a good position himself he would try to lay on the perfect chance for a better-placed colleague.

It was not so much unselfishness on Haynes' part. It arose because of his attitude to the game. He was a perfectionist and he always sought to carve out the perfect opening. Because he was still that same perfectionist he did not enjoy shooting unless he was sure the ball would go in. He certainly would not enjoy missing a goal chance.

If I had been lucky enough to have been his manager I would have encouraged him to shoot at every opportunity, and his scoring record, not a bad one by any means, would have been far more impressive.

Haynes' unfailing claim to greatness is that when people in football start talking about outstanding passers of the through ball they only mention one name.

Haynes was born in the reaches of North London so close to White Hart Lane that he should have been a natural capture for Tottenham. Ironically, his 'home' club admired him throughout his career. Yet, he stayed loyal to unfashionable Fulham.

That he chose Fulham was due in no small way to Tosh Chamberlain, the left-winger who had joined the Thames-side club in 1949. Tosh had been a schoolboy pal of Johnny, and after playing superbly in England Schoolboys' 1950 win over Scotland, it seemed natural for Haynes to follow his mate to Craven Cottage.

He made his League debut on Boxing Day 1952 – the first of more than 700 games he was to play for Fulham, the majority of them in the same forward line as myself.

John made his international debut during his third season with the club – and scored the first of the 18 goals he was to collect in his 56 matches for England.

Fulham finally won promotion to the First Division in 1959. Two years later, with the maximum wage removed, Johnny became the first man in football to earn £100 a week. He was the first because our chairman, Tommy Trinder, insisted he deserved to be.

It was no secret that this dramatic wage rise kept Haynes in England, when the lure of Italy – having already claimed a number of his contemporaries – was pulling very strongly.

John, however, was at that time an automatic choice in an England side enjoying its finest run for years. Under Walter Winterbottom, and captained by Haynes,

they were unbeaten for the first six internationals of the 1960-61 season, scoring 40 goals and conceding eight.

Not surprisingly, Haynes himself always insists that the best England performance he was ever a part of was the 9-3 massacre of Scotland, during that memorable sequence of results.

It is impossible to say quite what heights John may have touched, or how long he would have maintained them, but for the 1962 car crash in Blackpool. It put him out of all football for a year, and he never regained his England place, despite a press campaign for his return during 1964.

In July, 1964, Tottenham had lost one of the mainsprings of their glory years when John White was killed by lightning. Manager Bill Nicholson urgently needed a replacement creator. Haynes was the man he wanted.

Nicholson offered £90,000 but the deal was never completed, possibly robbing Johnny Haynes of the club honours he never achieved in English football.

When he retired in 1970, the English game lost one of its masters of passing – the simple skill accomplished with a polished ease that delighted spectators and embarrassed full-backs.

He took his talents to South Africa, and oddly enough, helped Durban City to the League title. A medal at last.

Harry Hibbs

England, Birmingham

Hibbs was a name from the past to conjure with when I was a lad. I soon learned that Harry Hibbs was one of England's outstanding goalkeepers between the two World Wars. He was built on the small side but lack of inches rarely handicapped him and I recall in one of my earliest scrapbooks that I had a photograph of Hibbs clutching the ball off the head of a Scottish forward during an international match. Somehow it epitomised all that I had been told about his goalkeep-

Small but good, Harry Hibbs was England's regular and dependable goalkeeper in the 1930s.

ing. There was nothing flamboyant about his saves, none of the acrobatic and sometimes needless athletic feats of modern-day 'keepers, particularly those from Continental countries. He could make the fiercest-directed shot into a comfortable catch simply by skilled positioning. No doubt he learned much from Dan Tremelling, another Birmingham goalkeeper who played for England, for Hibbs was a dedicated young man, quiet to the point of timidity until he pulled that 'keeper's jersey over his head. From that moment he commanded his area with unquestioned authority. Eddie Hapgood, who captained England during the 1930s, used to say that Hibbs developed such a rapport with his defence that he knew exactly when it was his ball, no matter how confused the scene might be around him.

Hibbs was born at Wilnecote in Staffordshire country and progressed to Birmingham from Tamworth in the summer of 1924. He served a faithful apprenticeship until finally succeeding Tremelling and won the first of his 25 caps against Wales at Stamford Bridge in November, 1929, when George Camsell scored a hat-trick in England's 6-0 win.

He took part in a number of notable England performances including a 4-3 victory over the Austrian *Wunderteam* who arrived at Stamford Bridge in December, 1932, with an impressive ten-match unbeaten run which contained such victims as Scotland (5-0), Germany (6-0 and 5-0), Switzerland (8-1) and Hungary (8-2).

His contribution to Birmingham can be gauged from the fact that between 1929 and 1940 he played 340 League games, in addition to Cup and other matches. I am sure that one of his disappointments was losing the 1931 FA Cup final 2-1 to Midland neighbours, West Bromwich Albion, then a Second Division side.

Hibbs managed Walsall for a period and while there he helped in the development of Bert Williams who was to achieve fame for Wolves and England–as a goalkeeper.

Nandor Hidegkuti

Hungary, MTK Budapest

It is given to few players to change the course of football history, but Hidegkuti has every reason for regarding himself as one of them.

He came to Wembley in November, 1953, a spare, slim Hungarian wearing a No. 9 shirt on his back as England lined up to protect their record of never having been beaten at home by a foreign side.

Ninety agonising minutes later, humiliated English football fans had realised that Hidegkuti was not a spearhead centre-forward but a cross between that role and an old-style attacking centre-half. More than that, Hidegkuti played from side to side, just to confuse everybody.

He also knocked in three of Hungary's goals as they thrashed England with new-think soccer to the extent of six goals to three.

He will never be forgotten by fans who saw him. He was a different kind of centre-forward. He had the traditional speed. He had the expected shot like a mule. But he also had a passing ability that the British had not been brought up to expect from leaders of their attacks.

He could also read the game, and soon switched on to the fact that the English defence was marking by numbers. So he strolled, between scoring goals, away from the centre of action, was followed by the England centre-half, and left great gaps for his inside-forwards, Sandor Kocsis and Ferenc Puskas, to surge through like a pair of stormtroopers.

That great Hungarian team, Olympic champions in 1952 and beaten in the final of the 1954 World Cup rather unluckily by West Germany, was one of the greatest teams of all times. It had six world class players, and Hidegkuti was one of them.

The idea of the withdrawn centre-forward was taken up all round the soccer-playing world and if the battering-ram centre-forward was not immediately killed off, then Wembley was where they started saying the last rites.

The idea was a combination of brains, but it would not, could not, have worked if the Hungarians had not had somebody of Hidegkuti's ability.

Hidegkuti, later to become a respected coach, was technically equipped for any type of role. He went to Sweden for the 1958 World Cup, but played in only the first match. The Hungary team was in the process of being patched up after the 1956 revolution. Hidegkuti was one of the players who stayed at home. He was a one-club man to the end.

Emlyn Hughes

England, Blackpool, Liverpool

The choice of Emlyn Hughes among the greatest footballers may surprise a lot of folk who consider themselves shrewd judges. Certainly he is no Georgie Best, but look what Liverpool won under his captaincy and consider what the Hughes influence must have been at Anfield.

Nandor Hidegkuti (left) playing for Hungary against West Germany in the 1954 World Cup finals.

European trophies, Cup medals at home, First Division titles, Emlyn must be one of the most decorated players in the game. Can it all be just coincidence and ten other players?

He has also taken time off from his Anfield duties to amass more than half a century of caps for England including, would you believe, a number of matches as skipper.

His stamina is extraordinary. His commitment to the cause, whether Liverpool's or England's, is remarkable. And, in a first-class career that began in 1965 and despatched him from Blackpool to Liverpool two years later as a 19-year-old worth £65,000 on the transfer market, the number of indifferent games is hardly worth counting.

His nickname, cheerfully bestowed from the Kop, is 'Crazy Horse'. A lot of so-called captains could do with Emlyn's sort of sanity because it gets players going. An effective player does not always have to be flamboyant and that is not Emlyn's style.

He is such a good defender whether at left-back, where he operates more frequently, or in the left centre-back position

97

A dedicated captain of Liverpool and England, Emlyn Hughes clears from Martin Peters of Spurs.

which he prefers, that it becomes a problem for any opponent to get the ball past him. When the opponent tries to get himself through as well as the ball, the situation is virtually impossible.

It is often said of the Liverpool skipper that because he is a big fellow he is not so fast when he is turned. Again, I insist that when Emlyn is beaten he usually finds the pace to make a decent tackle before the ball can be crossed.

I have also heard it argued that he is not so good in the air. He is 5ft 10½in tall so how good do you have to be? It is only once in a

while that anybody beats him upstairs and gets a goal out of it.

He has played orthodox midfield occasionally, especially in his earlier days, and he is not a bad operator there, either.

He is powerful in the manner of Duncan Edwards. He may not be quite as accurate as Duncan in his passing, but he is more reliable than his detractors will have people believe.

Emlyn is not a devious player. When he makes a blunder, everybody on the ground sees it. That is what stays in the onlookers' minds and blinds them to his general effectiveness.

A perfect captain never knows when he is beaten, and Emlyn has been a non-stop driving force first at the centre and then the head of affairs at Anfield since 1967. For what Liverpool have achieved in the years since I would give no Liverpool player any more credit than Emlyn.

He has not done badly considering that he is the son of a Welsh Rugby League international, born in Barrow but now as Scouse as they make them.

He was Footballer of the Year in 1977 which surprised nobody because Liverpool missed the golden treble of European Cup, First Division Championship and FA Cup probably only by a deflected Manchester United goal in the FA Cup final.

After the European triumph in Rome when Liverpool beat Moenchengladbach 3-1 to nail the European Cup at last, Emlyn was asked: 'What can you do to follow that?'

The answer came back in best Hughes tradition. It was: 'Win it again'.

Geoff Hurst

England, West Ham United, Stoke City, West Bromwich Albion

Geoff Hurst was one of the most underestimated footballers of our time, a far better

A Geoff Hurst speciality was the leap above the defence and the well-directed header.

player than most people realised. Of course he scored three goals in the final of the World Cup, a feat in itself that guarantees him immortality. But scoring goals on a big occasion is one thing; creating a new style of forward play for others to copy as a pattern for the future is another.

Hurst did just that, and there lies the reason for his unique slot in football history. Target man is an easy glib phrase that rolls off the tongue these days. Yet, without Hurst, it is not certain that there would be such a type of player.

The former West Ham wing-half perfected the role of an attacker running free to pick up balls played to him out of defence, and then turning to inflict the maximum amount of damage. It sounds easy, but it is not.

For a start, there is a vast amount of running involved in becoming available at all times for passes from defence. It takes a highly developed football brain and an unselfish streak, too, to perform it well.

The professionals call it the art of push-ball running, and there are very few plaudits to be won doing the job because not many average fans really appreciate what the target man is trying to do. It is also a lonely occupation. Most of the target man's colleagues are back in their own half when he gets the ball played up to him.

It takes a special breed even to attempt the job, and Hurst was one of them. Tall and well-muscled, Hurst had the ideal physique for the role and had the knack of being able to use his body perfectly to hold off opponents when passing or shooting.

The fact that Hurst was not built for speed was not necessarily a disadvantage. Because of it he had to use his brain to create greater opportunities for himself. But he was blessed with a powerful shot in either foot.

I was one of the few people who did not disagree entirely when Sir Alf Ramsey preferred Hurst to Jimmy Greaves in his World Cup side for the final against West Germany.

I do not think it any discredit to Greaves, who was a different type of player, to suggest that Hurst, in that particular team, added another ingredient, the capacity to pull defenders out of position by a stream of effective runs throughout 90 minutes.

Now there are some players who run for the sake of it. Geoff Hurst knew just how and where to run to create fear and panic in the opposing defence. That asset provides so many opportunities for other players that it is invaluable.

Hurst led the field in this art. So far, none of his successors have reached his standard. Perhaps that is not so unexpected for Hurst had excellent control of the ball. He used his chest probably as effectively as any other player in the game and his perfect laybacks made him a marvellous player to have on any side.

Hurst was a natural all-rounder. His father Charlie Hurst was a centre-half of Third Division standard, and Geoff himself could easily have become an Essex county cricketer. He played for the second XI several times before deciding that soccer had more to offer him. And that wasn't a bad decision, either.

Six youth caps in 1959 were followed by a professional contract at West Ham where it was manager Ron Greenwood who first saw Hurst, who was by no means an exceptional performer in midfield, as the player who might make something of a new idea he had.

Between 1959 and 1972 Hurst turned it all on for West Ham. He clocked up 410 League games which brought him 180 goals. England capped him 49 times and drew a dividend of 24 goals. If ever a man looked tied to a team for life, it was Hurst.

Then he decided to ask for a transfer, purely on the grounds that he had been there too long. He needed a new challenge, a fresh interest.

So Tony Waddington, then the Stoke manager who specialised in signing mature stars from other clubs, parted with £80,000 and got one of the most honest professionals in the game.

Hurst was glad to go to the Potteries. Staffordshire gave him a chance to expand his business interests, and though Hurst's days of glory were now past, both he and Stoke got their money's worth from each other.

A dozen games for West Bromwich Albion, when they were trying to get out of the Second Division under Johnny Giles, convinced honest Hurst that it was time to call it a day.

He accepted an offer from Southern League Telford to become their manager, and he was one of the first Ron Greenwood turned to for help when he became England manager.

Hurst will always have a contribution to make to English soccer.

David Jack

England, Plymouth Argyle,
Bolton Wanderers, Arsenal

Bob Wall, that doyen of soccer administrators, has often recounted how Herbert Chapman and he conspired to establish the first five-figure transfer deal which brought David Jack from Bolton to Arsenal in October, 1928. Wall, then in his first year as personal assistant to Chapman, remembers how the wine waiter was instructed to give the Bolton directors as much spirits as they wanted while ensuring that the glasses of the two Arsenal representatives at the negotiations contained only tonic water and ginger ale. Gradually, as a feeling of well-being spread over them, the Bolton party agreed to sell Jack for a fee of £10,890. How well the money was spent can be seen from Jack's accomplishments with the 'Gunners'. In 1930 he gained his third FA Cup winners' medal and he played an important part in the Championship successes of 1930-31 and 1932-33.

David Jack acquired his early soccer training while on the books of Plymouth

David Jack in training for the 1923 Cup Final. He scored the first goal at Wembley.

Argyle, who were managed by his father. He moved to Bolton Wanderers in 1920 and three years later scored Bolton's first goal in the 2-0 defeat of West Ham United in Wembley's opening FA Cup final. A crowd estimated at a quarter of million arrived at the ground, although the official attendance was 126,047, and there were frightening scenes as part of the vast crowd spilled on to the pitch. The game was delayed for 40 minutes and Jack's goal was scored in the second minute while a West Ham player was struggling to get back on the pitch after tumbling into the massed ranks on the touchlines.

In 1926 Jack and Bolton were back at Wembley—and once again he scored, what proved to be the only goal of the game against Manchester City. After moving south to Highbury, Jack helped Arsenal to beat Huddersfield Town 2-0 in the 1930 Final but his luck turned when Newcastle triumphed 2-1 at Wembley two years later.

Jack came from a family steeped in soccer. His brothers David and Donald played with him both at Plymouth Argyle and at Bolton and this influential pedigree shone through as he mesmerised opposing defences. He could be deceptively relaxed one moment, a fearsome adversary the next when he took his tall frame elegantly into striking range with a lazy-looking body swerve. The effectiveness of his shooting makes an emphatic statistic: 261 goals from 1920 to 1934.

He won nine caps, four with Bolton and five while with Arsenal. His last appearance proved a high-note for England as their 4-3 triumph at Stamford Bridge in December, 1932, ended a sequence of ten unbeaten games by Austria's *Wunderteam*.

Alec Jackson

Scotland, Aberdeen, Huddersfield, Chelsea
Some men achieve immortality by corporate deeds; Alec Jackson entered soccer's legends in one afternoon. He was a member of that most famous of Scottish teams—for ever after to be dubbed 'The Wembley Wizards'—which annihilated England to the tune of five goals to one at Wembley in the Home International Championship of 1928. Alec

Alec Jackson (right) with Hughie Gallacher, both Chelsea and Scotland.

Jackson, at 5ft 7in, was easily the tallest of the tiny Scottish forward line which bemused and befuddled a team of proven class. Four of his Huddersfield colleagues were in the England side and how they must have wished, long before the final whistle, that Jackson had stayed in Huddersfield! For he scored a brilliant hat-trick which illustrated both his speed off the mark and the stinging punch in his feet.

Herbert Chapman, that master manager of Huddersfield and Arsenal, was attracted by Jackson's skills on the right wing for Aberdeen and persuaded him to leave his native heath in 1925. Jackson's all-round gifts played a not inconsiderable part in Huddersfield completing a hat-trick of League Championship titles. But fortune smiled less favourably on Jackson and the Town club in the FA Cup. They lost 3-1 to Blackburn, despite Jackson's goal, in 1928, and two years later they went down 2-0 to Arsenal, by this time managed by Chapman.

Subsequently Jackson joined Chelsea but this was not a happy period for him and a dispute led to his departure from the League scene at the comparatively early age of 27.

He played 17 times for Scotland between 1925 and 1930 and although the 1928 match was the highlight of his international career, Jackson delivered another knock-out blow to England two years earlier when he scored the only goal of the match at Manchester.

In all League appearances—a total of 278, he reached a century of goals.

Jairzinho

Brazil, Botafogo

Back in 1970, when he fired most of the bullets in Brazil's World Cup triumph, Jairzinho was the most feared right-winger on the globe.

As Brazil surged on to what was probably the most technically satisfying of their

Jairzinho (Brazil) is quick off the mark and appears to have caught Beckenbauer (West Germany) wrong-footed.

World Cup successes, the powerful Jairzinho scored in every match, a thundering human grenade along the right touchline.

Yet he never wanted to play in the position in which he was acknowledged as the world's No. 1.

For Jairzinho, born beneath the shadow of the man-made figure of Christ which dominates Rio de Janeiro, was a frustrated striker at heart. With seven goals in six Mexico matches, nobody would have understood why he yearned to be the central striker.

Jairzinho and Garrincha go down in history as Brazil's magnificent No. 7s. The Little Bird was a natural. Jairzinho, cold and calculating, was not. He played on the wing only because he was too good to be left out of the side, and there were a couple of characters named Pelé and Tostao who had certain claims to the glamorous striking positions.

Jairzinho knew how they felt. He had gone from the suburbs of Rio to Botafogo in 1961 as a youthful right-winger but could not get into the side because national hero Garrincha was holding down that position.

So for the club, Jairzinho, whose shooting power could never be relegated to a reserve team, moved inside, and liked it. He had the freedom to roam, the freedom to come at goalkeepers and surprise them from unexpected angles, the wider freedom to unleash those explosive assaults on goal.

He was also one of the most intelligent players ever to don the famous yellow shirt of Brazil. After Garrincha returned home the hero of Chile 1962, Jairzinho worked on to make himself indispensable to the national squad. He achieved it. Both he and Garrincha came to Britain for the 1966 World Cup.

Both played in the first match, with Jairzinho on the left touchline. He had proved his point. He could not be left out. Both were there for the second game in which Hungary) inflicted on Brazil their

first World Cup defeat for 12 years. Both were left out of the third and final match . . . but Jairzinho came back.

Brazil should have known better than to banish him to the left-wing. He had won his first cap in 1964. They were not experimenting with an untried youngster.

By 1970, Brazil had got it as right as they could, allowing that Jairzinho, Tostao and Pelé had got to be the front three. Not that Jairzinho needed then to worry overmuch about the football. He was one of the best players in the world and the money was rolling in.

True to character, Jairzinho took no chances in business. Just as he did on the field he played the percentages. No risks. Straight into investments. Subsequently Jairzinho retired one of the richest of players.

That surprised nobody. All that he gave away in Mexico was space, acres of it down

104

the right wing as he drifted naturally into the centre. It was down that right-wing corridor that skipper Carlos Alberto constantly tore to destroy the Italians in the 1970 final.

Back to Botafogo, with whom he had won several League championship medals, went Jairzinho, back into the central striker position.

In his third World Cup, West Germany 1974, Jairzinho finally got the job he wanted, leading the Brazil attack. Ironically, compared with Mexico, he played in six games and scored only twice.

It is not given to many of us to achieve fame despite ourselves. Jairzinho is one of the few. He is one of the truly exceptional strikers of a ball, and a natural winger, even though he might argue about it.

Remarkably, Jairzinho achieved his peak against the odds. Twice in 1967 he broke his right leg, and that followed a bone trans-

plant in the same leg. Yes, his right leg, the limb Jairzinho used for centering and firing cannons.

Apart from ball control, taken for granted with almost any Brazilian, Jairzinho revealed courage of the highest order. All the worst left-backs in the world bruised him. There was hardly one who did not live to regret it, made to look stupid by a yellow express train that roared past them and was later identified as a human being named Jairzinho.

Alex James

Scotland, Raith Rovers, Preston North End, Arsenal

To grow up in the London suburb of Balham as I did in the 1930s was to know only one soccer hero–Alex James, a tiny miracle man

Alex James in untypical role–going up with Middlesbrough goalkeeper Hillier for a corner.

who played inside-left for Arsenal and was the football star we all wanted to emulate.

What then was the magic of James? To the boys he was a little man who could make the big fellows look fools by sheer skill alone. To the adult football fan he had an ability to dribble and a bodyswerve that marked him as a man apart.

He also had, in modern vernacular, charisma. Headlines did not make James. James made headlines.

He was a player of extremes. He was either leaving sprawling and embarrassed defenders behind him. Or being snubbed by Scotland for reasons only the selectors of that time could begin to answer.

In 1929-30, his first season with Arsenal, James won three caps. In the next five seasons during which Arsenal once managed to flop into second place while winning the First Division title four times, the Scots capped James just once. He who said that there ain't no justice must have had wee Alex in mind.

Centre parting, baggy pants and exquisite ball control–that was Alex James.

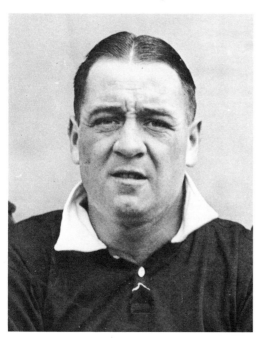

Despite his marvellous skills, James has lingered in the memory as much for his appearance as for anything else. Seldom has football thrown up a star to delight the cartoonists quite as James did.

Through his years in the game, Alex was caricatured first in those outrageous golfing plus-fours, then in the equally baggy and astonishingly long shorts he wore onfield, and finally as the dapper, smart-suited Londoner he was to become as a Highbury hero.

This, though, was to come later. He began at Raith Rovers, hardly Britain's most fashionable club, and stayed there for three years, until Preston parted with £3,250 to acquire his signature in September, 1925.

By then, Alex was already 23, so scarcely an impetuous youngster making his debut in the English League. Preston found him no instant miracle-maker, however, losing 5-1 to Middlesbrough when he took his place in their side for the first time.

Defeats followed in two further away matches, before Alex finally produced what he was capable of in his home debut. After six games, he had scored six goals. Preston was buzzing.

He finished top scorer that season, with 14 goals, but Preston stayed in the Second Division due to a poor away record. The next season they finished sixth, but in 1927-28 it seemed they would finally go up.

For much of the season, they contested the top spot with Manchester City, and when the teams were due to meet, at Maine Road in February, Alex was confronted with a club against country situation. Scotland had picked him to play against Ireland, but James chose to stay and help Preston. He gave one of his finest shows ever in a 2-2 draw–but still, Preston were to falter and finish fourth.

Early the following season, Preston were again approached to release James for an international. This time, they kept quiet, but Alex discovered the truth. Relations between the club and their star were never the same again, and in 1929, having refused a move to Manchester City, he joined Arsenal for £8,750.

James had scored 53 goals in 146 games for Preston, where he had been allowed a free rein to express his talents and enjoy himself. All that was to change at Arsenal.

Manager Herbert Chapman decided, in his own words, that Alex should 'cut out the circus tricks'. He was employed in a deeper role, directing the legendary attack that was at first comprised of Hulme, Jack, Lambert and Bastin. His goals became irregular surprises.

He was probably reluctant to sacrifice the personality that had so endeared him to Preston fans; but he accepted his new role, and accomplished it superbly.

Arsenal won the League Championship four times between 1931 and 1935, and took the FA Cup in 1930 and 1936. James retired in 1937, and when he died at the age of 51, in 1953, he left a vision of cheeky, irrepressible talent that was to be treasured by all who saw him and craved by many who did not.

Pat Jennings

Northern Ireland, Watford,
Tottenham Hotspur, Arsenal

With so much ability and so much modesty to go with it, that it is a wonder the two can mould together, Pat Jennings is a gentle goalkeeping giant. A most likeable person, he is so gentle‘and calm that forwards almost want to apologise when they jump with him for a cross.

Born with a huge pair of hands and the same sort of confidence as Danny Blanchflower, he combines his innate modesty with the belief that as the hands were God-given with which to catch the ball he might just as well do it.

For a big man, standing 6ft and weighing over 13st, Jennings is extremely quick at making reaction saves on the line, perhaps as good as any goalkeeper when confronted with a forward breaking through on his own.

Footballer of the Year, 1973–Pat Jennings (Tottenham Hotspur).

It is then that Jennings is revealed at his best, spreading himself so well along the ground to block a shot or to anticipate any other course of action by the opposing forward.

High crosses he will take so sweetly with two hands, and occasionally, just to show what is possible, he will pick a ball out of the air with one hand.

A goalkeeper needs to be confident when he comes for crosses. Judgement must be sound and Jennings has this attribute in full measure.

He is an exceptionally long kicker of a ball, and I think this is much more important than is generally realised. The right kind of kicking puts pressure on the opposing defence immediately.

Though some people think every move should be built up gradually, starting from the goalkeeper, I am not among them. I think an equally effective way is to power long kicks against a defence that might well be destroyed by that method of attack.

In Jennings' early days at Tottenham, the London club had two tall strikers, Martin Chivers and Alan Gilzean. It was one of the sights of White Hart Lane, a huge Jennings' clearance that either took on his head almost on the edge of the other team's penalty area.

Jennings owes his exceptional kicking ability to having played a lot of Gaelic football back home in Newry, and it once enabled him to get on the Spurs' score sheet. Playing against Manchester United in the FA Charity Shield match in 1967, he cleared from his own penalty area. With the wind behind it, the ball bounced in the United area where goalkeeper Alex Stepney misjudged it. Jennings would certainly have felt very sorry for his opposite number.

Jennings made his first appearance at Wembley as long ago as 1963 as a member of the Irish Youth team. A few days later, former Spurs skipper Ron Burgess, then managing Watford, gambled £6,000 on him.

Within months, with technique and physique improving parallel to each other, it was obvious that Jennings was not going to stay long at Watford. Nor did he.

He made his debut in 1963, played the one full season in 1963-64, and then went to Tottenham for £27,500, a sizeable fee for a goalkeeper then, and a good return on Watford's gamble.

Spurs boss Bill Nicholson was in the process of rebuilding his side three years after the 1960-61 double. For a couple of seasons Jennings disputed the position with Bill Brown, the Scottish international, and then he made it his own.

Until 1976 Jennings had no challenger. Then Barry Daines arrived and Spurs were

Pat Jennings stretches to push a shot round the post.

in the same position as Leicester when the youthful Shilton came along to challenge the established Banks.

Just as Leicester kept the younger man, so did Spurs. Jennings was priced modestly and allowed to sign for rivals Arsenal, for whom he played against Ipswich in the FA Cup final of 1978, far from finished.

The 'gift' transfer was no more than Jennings deserved. He had given Spurs tremendous service, playing more games for the club than any other player.

He had won an FA Cup winner's medal when they beat Chelsea in the 1967 final, he had been in the League Cup winning side against Aston Villa in 1971, and he had propped them up in Europe.

But in 1976-77, a season of injuries for him, he and Daines could not keep Spurs in the First Division. It seemed right that a goalkeeper of his stature was transferred before he needed to play a Second Division game.

Ireland first named him as goalkeeper in 1964 when he was still at Watford. Eventually he left the record of 59 Northern Ireland caps by former Arsenal and Hull centre-half Terry Neill way behind.

He was Footballer of the Year in 1972-73, and never has there been a more popular choice. After Banks's career was ended, Jennings was generally regarded as the best goalkeeper in the world. But that was a subject Jennings would never discuss.

Cliff Jones

Wales, Swansea Town, Tottenham Hotspur, Fulham

Cliff Jones was to Tottenham and Wales what Stanley Matthews and Tom Finney were to England – quite a beautiful artist. What made Cliff, small and slight, was his uninhibited bravery.

A fast moving direct winger, able to play on either flank, his most devastating ploy was courageously to run the ball into the penalty area, right in among the flying feet

Cliff Jones blasts in a shot and Ron Springett flinches, Spurs v Sheffield Wednesday, 1960.

which even he could not always dodge.

He had exceptional balance. He could feint and weave, change direction and pace, and disguise his intentions all the time he was doing it. And he would go in and head where it hurts because with Jones' size against him there was often no way he could avoid bruises in heading battles.

A player steeped in the tradition of Spurs, and a key member of the League and Cup double-winning side, had to be able to play a bit, too, so Jones was a long way from being a head-down dribbler with no vision.

Once he got into a position when the opposing defence had been put into confusion, then Jones was composed enough to ensure that the final pass was a killer.

Fast, blazing wingers of the Jones type, able to go either side of a full-back, never did come very often. It seems a great pity that they were temporarily phased out of the modern game.

Cliff may have been the most famous footballer to emerge from the village of Penyard in the Merthyr Valley. He was far from being the only one.

Brothers, cousins and uncles, all from this tiny, rather depressing Welsh village, form a footballing clan that make the Joneses very hard to keep up with.

Cliff was the son of Ivor Jones and nephew of Bryn – both Welsh internationals in their own right – but he was to become greater than either.

His career began at Swansea, near his birthplace, where, for a short while, he played in the same team as his brother, Bryn, and cousin Ken. Cliff, however, was destined to be the real success of the second generation Jones footballers.

Cliff made his first appearance for Wales before he had played in 30 League games. In all, he played 168 times for Swansea, before being sold to Tottenham in February of 1958.

The fee was a record for the Welsh club and, for some months, the load weighed

heavily on Cliff Jones' shoulders.

He scored only once in the ten remaining matches that season, and when he broke a leg in a practice match in August, 1958, he may have begun to regret the move completely.

For Wales, though, Cliff just got better and better, and he played in all five World Cup matches as they surprisingly reached the last eight in the 1958 tournament.

The broken leg kept him out for five months. He returned to a Tottenham team that was being rapidly and successfully reshaped by Bill Nicholson and Danny Blanchflower. Cliff was to play a crucial part in the glory years to come.

In the next ten seasons, he scored almost 200 goals as Tottenham swept the board. Cliff won three FA Cup winners medals, one from the League Championship and one from the European Cup-Winners Cup.

He was one of the last of an era. An era when wingers went for goal, directly and bravely. Courage was Cliff's hallmark, matched by astonishing speed and acro-

A typical Cliff Jones headed goal–this one against Nottingham Forest in 1962.

batic heading that belied his 5ft 7in frame. He scored many goals by going in for a ball that others would have ignored. Inevitably, he was often injured.

In late 1968, Tottenham paid a fitting gesture to this wonderful servant when they gave him a free transfer. Fulham took on the ageing wing master, but he played only another 25 club games before retiring. While at Fulham, however, he added two further Welsh caps, making a total of 59 that only Ivor Allchurch has bettered.

Kevin Keegan

England, Scunthorpe United, Liverpool, SV Hambourg

It may sound like extravagant praise, but Keegan, in one way, is like Pelé. He has such marvellous physical attributes, such strength, compressed into his small frame.

That is what gives him his special

character as a footballer because I would not say he is one of the great ball-playing artists in the game. On the other hand there is the old football truism that it is not how, but how many. And that is certainly true of Keegan.

It is all about how many goals you score, how many opponents for whom you make life miserable or even impossible, how many chances you create from nothing, how many balls you win in the air no matter what your height . . . all those things Keegan gets involved in.

Though Keegan's 5ft 8in and only 10½st physique might be expected to be against him as a penalty-area powerhouse, he is tougher than most. This means he can be particularly effective in the European vendetta games. He cannot be kicked out of them. He has the strength to take the knocks and at the end it is usually his opponents' nerves that are shattered and not his.

The alert Keegan, developed to complete maturity after a season's experience on the Continent, is one of the world's best takers of half-chances. He is so quick. He strikes like a snake with either head or foot, so fast that he almost beats the eye.

Because of the spring in his heels he can jump half a dozen inches higher than seems possible and consequently catches out many a defender who reckons Keegan has no chance of getting to the ball.

I've seen big defenders still going lazily for a ball that Keegan has just flicked off their heads and down for a marauding colleague.

Keegan also has tremendous stamina. He can run himself into the ground in the cause of the team, as he proved on the memorable night in Rome when Liverpool won the European Cup by beating Moenchengladbach 3-1.

That was the performance that clinched

Kevin Keegan came to Liverpool from Scunthorpe and quickly made the Kop his own.

his half million pounds transfer to Hambourg in the summer of 1977.

In all the years since Keegan made the highest grade, there have been arguments about whether he is better played as a striker or in midfield.

I prefer to see him up front. In midfield he will get through a lot of work but at his peak form he should be up there in the thick of it scoring goals. I think he loves to play there, doing what comes naturally and most effectively, creating goals from impossible situations.

Temperamentally, there are no doubts about Keegan. He was an instant star, and coped with the pressures of Anfield and the Kop's adulation quite easily.

He arrived at Anfield from Fourth Division Scunthorpe in 1971, bought just before Liverpool lost the FA Cup final 2-1 to Arsenal. It was a transfer typical of the way manager Bill Shankly was operating at that time, scouring the Fourth Division for cheap talent, prospecting for gold among the nuggets.

Normally, Shankly played them in Liverpool's reserve teams for a couple of seasons to pick up the Liverpool method. But, uncharacteristically, he threw in Keegan on the opening day of the 1971-72 season.

He was an instant sensation. Apart from injuries, Keegan was never left out of the Anfield side until his departure for Hambourg six summers later when English domestic football lost one of its few world class players.

It was six years of glory for the lad from Doncaster. In that time, the modest Keegan won three First Division championship medals, a European Cup winner's medal, medal, two EUFA Cup winner's medals, and an FA Cup winner's medal. There were failures. Once Liverpool lost the FA Cup final and twice they finished only second in the First Division!

Keegan was an established star. Happy on Merseyside, or so it seemed, where he ruled.

Keegan bursts through two Leeds players in the FA Charity Shield match of 1974.

But the Yorkshireman, rejected by Coventry when he was a schoolboy, was getting frustrated.

He shook Liverpool fans by saying that he wanted to leave Anfield. And was honest enough to say that he had no more mountains to conquer in British soccer. He wanted to test his skill on the Continent.

Captain of Cardiff and Wales in their successful days in the 1920s, Fred Keenor with the FA Cup, 1927.

Liverpool saw his point, and his eye for business. He knew he was bordering on greatness. By the late 1970s so did the rest of the soccer world.

Fred Keenor

Wales, Cardiff City, Crewe Alexandra

One of the more favoured questions set in sports quiz programmes must be: when was the FA Cup taken out of England? The man who masterminded that feat was Fred Keenor, who captained Cardiff City in 1927 when they defeated Arsenal 1-0 at Wembley and so removed the trophy to Wales for the first time in the history of the competition.

The Principality owes much to the industry and example of such early pioneers as Keenor. This native of Cardiff joined the City club in 1913, just three years after it turned professional, and helped to guide them from the obscurity of the Southern League to First Division status in the Football League.

Those who saw Keenor during a League career which stretched from 1913 to 1934 are almost unanimous on one point–his

114

Sharp in the box, Denis Law typically gets a foot to the ball in a goalmouth mêlée against Coventry.

inspirational qualities of leadership. He may not have been a half-back of exceptional talent but there was no denying his driving power. Often by the magnetism of his personality he sparked fresh life into the team which, under his captaincy, rarely accepted defeat without an enormous challenge. And there were seasons of glory, too. In 1920-21 City were runners-up in the Second Division and three seasons later they finished level on points at the top of the First Division, only to be deprived of the Championship by Huddersfield Town who had a fractionally better goal average.

By that time Cardiff were such a force in the land beyond the valleys that in season 1925-26 they had as many as 17 players on their books who had played at international level.

Those were palmy days indeed for Wales and from 1932 to 1934 they won the Home International Championship for two seasons without suffering a single defeat. Needless to say, Keenor (who by then had moved to Crewe) was among those who represented them. In all, Keenor won 32 caps, the majority at centre-half, though he was equally efficient at right-half.

Cardiff have discovered and trained many players of greater flair than Fred Keenor but surely none who did more to establish the roots of the club. That is why I am delighted to include his name in this hall of fame.

Denis Law

Scotland, Huddersfield Town, Manchester City, Torino, Manchester United, Manchester City

Looking back at the ability of Denis Law, the two words that must come to anybody's mind are electric and quicksilver. Denis was an electronic, or even bionic, player, a devastating piece of goalscoring equipment beautifully designed to reach the ball before any other player and produce whatever movement was necessary to get it into the net.

But dashing Denis was a long way from being just a piece of machinery. Football fans the world over, and particularly those

Denis Law pounces, and slips the ball past the despairing dive of Everton's Gordon West.

north of the English border, adored the handsome, arrogant Scotsman.

He had the looks of Danny Kaye, and there was something of the clown in him, too. He was always ready, whatever the excitement or the stress, to break into that magnetic smile of his.

Denis could never be described as one of the world's great ball artists. I remember filming him for television when, because of the pressure and the excitement of the camera rolling, he had some difficulty in just keeping the ball up on his feet. Yet part of his superb ability was that he never made two movements when one would do.

So many of his best goals were scored with just one touch of the head or a flick with the foot with defenders wondering just where he had come from.

Law was very precise in his passing. I can see in my mind's eye now the picture of him concentrating on laying the ball back perfectly to a colleague. He was also one of those players who did everything twice as quickly and twice as accurately in places where it mattered. And for him that was in the opposition's goalmouth.

Law had one other supreme attribute. With him in the side no cause was ever lost. He was a picture of optimism to those off the field and the same influence was exerted on the field for every team in which he played.

He could be rated the perfect competitor, ever aware, ever determined, ever inventive, and never beaten. More than that, to relax when Denis was around was asking for trouble. Seldom did he give defenders a second chance.

Law's first chance came in the middle 1950s when he was sent down from the family home in Aberdeen to join

Huddersfield, a teenager wearing steel-rimmed spectacles. By the time he was 16 the super-confident Law was in the club's first team, directing players twice his age. He got away with it because he was that good, good enough for Matt Busby to offer £10,000 for him when he was still eligible for Huddersfield's youth team.

Busby was to make Law Scotland's youngest international at 18 years and seven months when he played him against Wales in 1958. Law was to go on until the 1974 World Cup, winning 55 caps and deserving many more.

Bill Shankly, then assistant-manager at Huddersfield, had a phrase for the young Law. It was, simply: 'The greatest thing on two feet'.

Eventually, Huddersfield had to sell Law. Busby had the chance to buy but Dennis Viollet and Bobby Charlton were playing so well at inside-forward at Old Trafford that Law was not approached.

Manchester City it was who handed over the then British record transfer fee of £55,000 in March, 1960, with City boss Les McDowall reckoning that he had signed another Raich Carter.

Law spent two seasons at Maine Road and was away again. Nobody could ever accuse Law of not knowing his own worth and there was a lot of lira to be made out of Italian soccer in 1961.

But the disciplines of Italian club life were not for Law. A year of frustration ended when Busby paid out yet another record fee, this time £115,000 to take Law to Old Trafford where he could have gone five years earlier.

Within a few matches, the Stretford End fans had christened him 'The King', and the title survived the challenge of George Best and stayed with him until 1973 when United let him go for a second spell with Manchester City. He was over the hill, anyway, they thought at Old Trafford. But he did enough at Maine Road to win back his Scotland place.

Those were the real glory days, through the 1960s at Old Trafford where he won First Division championship medals in 1964-65 and 1966-67, an FA Cup winner's medal in 1963 and the honour of being European Footballer of The Year in 1964.

Always a victim of injuries because of the furious style and pace at which he played, he was out of the side when Manchester United achieved their greatest triumph, the European Cup success in 1968.

But Law needs no medals to confirm his magic. All those who saw him will never forget that fiery packet of unique skills. Law is among Matt Busby's all time greats. That should be good enough for most people.

Tommy Lawton

England, Burnley, Everton, Chelsea,
Notts County, Brentford, Arsenal

If the average football fan in the 1940s had been asked to name the finest centre-forward who had ever played for England it is as likely as not that the answer would have been: Tommy Lawton.

For Tommy was the centre-forward who had everything: pace, power, heading ability out of this world, stamina, timing, the lot. Playing against Notts County, I once beat him in the air, and I thought I had jumped right out of the ground. That's how it felt to dominate him upstairs.

He was a master, with great vision in the air. Not only could he see the goals but he could see where the subtle deflections could be knocked down to other players.

He could pass well and hold the line together well, for those were the days when the No. 9 was expected to play well upfield.

He had a superb shot with either foot, and probably had it not been for the war he would have doubled his quota of England caps.

Lawton's future seemed secure from the time that he completed three seasons of Bolton schoolboy soccer with 570 goals to his name.

Tommy Lawton, in his Arsenal days in 1954, gets up to head for goal against Sheffield United at Highbury.

Scouts followed him like shadows. For, even at this stage, his immense heading ability was obvious and the shooting power, later to become so lethal, was developing fast.

Burnley won the race for his signature and hustled him into their League side while he was still 16–too young to sign professional forms. Then, four days after his 17th birthday, he scored a hat-trick against Spurs which effectively quashed any further argument. Tommy was bound for stardom.

Everton paid £6,500 for him a few months later–an extravagant fee for the day and an extraordinary one for a 17-year-old with only 25 League matches behind him.

They were not to regret the gamble. Lawton spent nine happy years at Goodison, albeit six of them war years, and helped them to the League Championship in 1939. That season, he scored 34 goals in 38 League games and won the first of his 23 official England caps.

Tommy served in the army during the war, and when it was over, he moved to London with his wife, signing for Chelsea for a record fee of £11,500.

His one full season there produced 26 goals in 34 games. Then Lawton's feet became itchy and Chelsea were eventually forced–very reluctantly–to part with their prize talent. His move to Notts County for £20,000 was a big soccer story. It was the first transfer to reach that sort of money–and it was paid by a club who were then in the Third Division.

Lawton played his last four internationals while with County, inspired their rise into the Second Division, and stayed at Meadow Lane until he was 33.

London beckoned once more, and Brentford was the next move. Most soccer people felt that this quiet Second Division backwater of the capital would be Lawton's grazing ground. So what happened next was a major sensation.

Early in the 1953-54 season, League champions Arsenal were enduring a shocking patch of eight games without a win. They needed an experienced man to general their raw forwards. They found him by buying 34-year-old Lawton.

For the best part of three seasons, he filled the role that manager Tom Whittaker had created for him. The speed was gone; so was some of the devastating power; the goal supply was not so plentiful. But Lawton was still talented and clever enough to bind his team-mates together. And the heading, that magical heading ability, that was still there, too.

Lawton and Arsenal parted amicably in 1956 and he went into management. Sadly, as has happened all too often, a great player did not become a great manager, and the man who scored goals at a rate that has seldom been matched in the game's history, faded quietly out of football.

Billy Liddell

Scotland, Liverpool

If Billy Liddell were playing today, there would not be a Scotland striker sure of his place in the national side–unless he were Liddell.

Tall, upright, strong, Liddell was made for today's style of attacking, and he had the courage to go in anywhere. He would chase any lost cause and no defender could settle while he was around.

Originally a left-winger, he was recommended to Liverpool by Sir Matt Busby when he was still a registered player at

Strong and fast, Billy Liddell was a part of the Liverpool forward line for 15 years.

Anfield, but because of the war he did not make his League debut until 1946 at the age of 24.

Good players did not fade away then. Liddell went on until he was 39, dominating the scene so much that when Liverpool were struggling in the middle 1950s they were frequently referred to as Liddellpool.

Liverpool went down from the First Division in 1954. But for Liddell's inspirational presence in the side they might easily have slipped through the trapdoor a season or so earlier.

Liddell liked to say he was an outside-left with the build of a centre-forward. Eventually he was needed in the middle.

That was not a problem. He had been

used to playing there in emergencies but preferred the space on the flanks. Liddell was less of a crafty winger than a direct player. Frills and finesse were not for him. It was speed that took him past defenders, and once he was in flight he was a very hard man to knock off the ball.

Stronger than most wingers, he was able to ride tackles well, but while there have certainly been cleverer ball manipulators, forwards do not often come with more determination.

Liddell was a model player. He was never in trouble, was booked only once in 20 years including wartime, and is still by far the most popular of all the old Anfield stars.

With canny Scottish upbringing, and remember that these were the days of maximum wages, Liddell always remained a part-time player supplementing his football income with work as an accountant.

Liddell, who won 28 Scottish caps to add to the eight he collected during the war, became to Liverpool what Tom Finney was to Preston.

The local image was perfect. Liddell later became bursar at Liverpool University, he was a Justice of the Peace, and he devoted hours of his spare time to youth work.

All the time he stayed one of Liverpool's greatest supporters, a shareholder and season-ticket holder.

Liddell's first season brought him a League championship medal, the only time Liverpool were to win the title in his playing days. He also got an FA Cup runners-up medal when the Anfield squad lost to Arsenal in 1950.

When Liddell retired in 1961 he took with him the distinction of having then played in more games for Liverpool than any other player. It was 492 League games plus 40 successive FA Cup ties and his haul of League goals came to 216.

One of them, incidentally, to demonstrate Liddell's power, was a header from outside the penalty area. The Scot's ball control was very good, but what most of his fellow professionals envied was his acceleration.

That was what made him so dangerous when he was switched to lead the Liverpool attack.

It was a desperation move really, reinforced by the knowledge that honest Liddell would be giving his usual 120 per cent. The 1950 Wembley team had disintegrated into relegation by 1954 and the attack was particularly unsettled.

Liddell went into the middle to pull it together. He succeeded up to a point, but Liverpool's trouble was that they could not find another Liddell type to do the same job at the back.

It was not surprising. Liddells are hard to find. As one of his former colleagues said: 'Billy could get goals out of nothing. And if he did not get one he always looked as though he could. He used to scare defenders rigid.'

Bill McCracken

Northern Ireland, Distillery,
Newcastle United

History will associate the name of Bill McCracken with the change in the offside law in 1925. Younger generations who have seen his name linked with this tactical alteration could be forgiven for thinking that McCracken was a leading administrator of his day, since law changes are matters for them rather than players. Yet, in fact, McCracken proved the fallibility of a system which had been in operation for almost 60 years by his pace and perception as a full-back with Newcastle United. He and his partner perfected such an understanding that they would move as close to the half-way mark as possible and often catch two or three forwards offside. The ploy was both effective and disruptive, so much so that clubs, administrators and the media began to complain that it was having a detrimental effect on the game as a spectator sport. So in 1925 the law was altered, on a proposal of the Scottish Football Association, that, in essence, a player shall not be offside if two (instead of three) opponents are nearer their own goal-line. And that, of course, is how the law has remained, though from time to time there have been experiments to restrict offside to one-third of the field at each end and adopting in those areas the old off-side law governed by three (instead of two) defenders.

Bill McCracken was born in 1883 and the skills which were to win him international recognition were first seen with Irish League club Distillery for whom he played between 1901 and 1904.

In February, 1902, he was capped for the first time at left-back against Wales in Cardiff when Northern Ireland marked their first match in the Welsh capital by winning 3-0. He played a further five internationals while with Distillery before, in 1904, Newcastle, in the face of eager competition from a number of Football League clubs, signed McCracken. Thus began a long and fruitful association at St James' Park in which he shared many of Newcastle's triumphs before the First World War. These included Football League Championship successes in 1906-07 and 1908-09 and an FA Cup winners' medal in 1909-10 when the 'Magpies' beat Barnsley 2-0 on Everton's ground, after a 1-1 draw at the old Crystal Palace. He also received FA Cup runners-up medals in 1908 (against Wolverhampton Wanderers) and 1911 (against Bradford City).

Considering his immense gifts as a full-back, capable of playing on either flank, McCracken ought to have won far more than 15 caps, but he was a man of strong opinions and frequently found himself at variance with the Irish Football Association on the question of finance. He felt, rightly or wrongly, that he was being underpaid and for a decade he was not considered for the national team. Happily, the passage of time and events softened attitudes on both sides and he was brought back in to the international fold in October, 1919. The occasion was an eagerly awaited match against

Big Bill McCracken in 1912, thirteen years before his full-back play forced a change in the off-side laws.

England in Belfast – the first official game between the countries since the end of the First World War. His partner at full-back was Bill McCandless, later to set up a remarkable record by taking three Welsh clubs, Newport, Cardiff and Swansea out of the Third Division.

The match ended in a 1-1 draw, and McCracken was in his 40th year when he made his final appearance in his country's colours against Scotland in Belfast in March, 1913.

When his playing career also closed that year, McCracken began more than a half century of service to the game as manager, coach and scout. He managed Hull City, Millwall and Aldershot and later became a much respected club scout, and was still watching potential talent for Watford when well into his nineties. Truly, a remarkable character who will always have his own special place in the story of the game.

Jimmy McGrory scored 410 League goals in 408 matches – the only goal-a-match man in British soccer.

Jimmy McGrory

Scotland, Celtic, Clydebank

'Have goals – will travel' is a catch phrase which has been used with varying degrees of optimism by some modern strikers. But for one player, above all others, the claim could have been made with utter validity. For Jimmy McGrory, who played in an era when deeds rather than words emphasised a man's worth, scored 550 goals in League, Cup and international matches. His incredible scoring feats brought him a total of 410 League goals during his career with Celtic and Clydebank – 397 of them for Celtic. No player has ever netted as many goals for a single British club. He finished top of the Scottish First Division list of goalscorers on three occasions and remains Celtic's most prolific marksman with 50 goals in the Scottish First Division in season 1935-36.

In one First Division match against Dunfermline in January, 1928, he scored eight goals for Celtic and eight years later,

in March, 1936, he achieved the rare distinction of getting three goals in the space of three minutes – a feat I suspect some headline writers of the present era would proclaim as a 'hot-trick'.

James Edward McGrory was a centre-forward in the classic mould. He was generously built, which enabled him physically to withstand, and indeed often topple, the challenges of defenders. He could collect a ball and slip an opponent with a sudden acceleration of pace, and I am told that his heading was comparable to that of Dixie Dean and Tommy Lawton in timing and power. All of which clearly made him a most respected adversary anywhere within striking range. Some cynical critics of past performances never cease to argue that these old-time marksmen would not have flourished in today's tight marking and frequently negative defensive set-ups.

My answer has always been that true talent would emerge in any period of the game's history. I prefer not to become involved in what, after all, is a pointless exercise, since the truth or otherwise of such contentions cannot be established.

Although he was undoubtedly the greatest goalscorer in Scottish football, McGrory never made a positive mark on the international scene. Possibly the most satisfying of his seven international appearances between 1928 and 1933 was his penultimate game against England in Glasgow in April, 1933, when he scored both goals in his country's 2-1 victory. On the face of it, these few matches in Scotland's colours do scant justice to the deadly finishing of McGrory but people who saw him play tend to reach the same conclusion: that he acquired almost telepathic understanding with the Celtic players and, naturally, this special relationship was not so much in evidence when he played occasional games for Scotland. He, of course, is not the first or indeed the last player to disappoint at national level when club credentials are exceptional.

He was a member of the Celtic team which won the Scottish Cup in 1925, 1931, 1933 and 1937. Twice too, he won Cup runners-up medals. He also took part in the successful Scottish League Championship quests by Celtic in 1925-26 and 1935-36.

McGrory turned to the managerial side of the game when his active career ended just before the Second World War. He was in charge first at Kilmarnock and then, from 1945 to 1965, he guided the destinies of his beloved Celtic.

Dave Mackay

Scotland, Heart of Midlothian, Tottenham Hotspur, Derby County, Swindon Town

Dave Mackay is just another way of saying aggression. There's a famous picture of Mackay glaring at Billy Bremner, hand gripping the front of Bremner's shirt and reducing his fellow Scot to the status of a schoolboy who has stepped out of line.

It is typical of Mackay, a born fighter, a born winner, and a man who refused to lie down and be counted out when he broke his left leg twice and consequently missed a season and a half.

Fate had a price to pay for inflicting that on Mackay. He extracted it by skippering Spurs to their 1967 FA Cup final 2-1 victory over Chelsea. Yet the magnitude of the man is reflected in the fact that captaining a Cup-winning side is, to Mackay, just another honour among so many.

Referee Norman Burtenshaw rushes up whistling as Dave Mackay (left) makes very threatening gestures at Billy Bremner in a Spurs v Leeds match.

Mackay started his career with Hearts in his native Edinburgh in 1953-54. When it ended at Swindon in 1972, he had played in 541 Scottish and Football League games, had scored 65 goals and won 22 Scotland caps, by no means as many as he should.

He had been Footballer of the Year in 1969, and collected practically every major honour going on both sides of the border.

But the greatest tributes to Mackay, the man and the player, do not shine from his trophy cabinet. They come from his fellow professionals.

Jimmy Greaves, his closest friend in the Spurs team, says: 'He was the greatest professional I ever played with. When he was missing we all had to work twice as hard. Many's the time I've looked up at the sky and been glad that he was playing with me and not against me.'

Alan Mullery, his wing-half partner at White Hart Lane, said after the second broken leg: 'Sheer guts got him back. I'm lost in admiration of the man.'

John Harvey, who was trainer of Hearts in Mackay's early playing days, recalls: 'We won five trophies the four years he was in the first team. He played like two men.'

Cliff Jones, Spurs winger, says: 'Once he settled into that No. 6 shirt he turned a good side into a great one.'

It is time now to nail the belief that Mackay's game was all physical. It was not, although he could bruise the side of a tank.

When he invariably used to come out of a tackle with the ball, the majority of us put it down to brute strength and guts.

It was obvious, when he started to slow down in his later years at Derby, and he was still coming out with the ball, that his timing must have been absolutely accurate. It was quite remarkable how he could read which way the ball or opponent was going and make a perfectly balanced tackle just at the right moment.

That skill is impossible to practise. It can only come from natural ability and vast experience.

Yet perhaps it does Mackay an injustice to make so much of his tackling. He was a very constructive player once he got the ball. His kicking, with both feet, was extremely good, and the sheer courage and vision of the man made him scorn the safe short pass if he could play an adventurous long ball.

I would not argue with anybody who said that Mackay was not the fastest player in the world. But when it came to picking up honours he was first to a few of those.

When Spurs manager Bill Nicholson paid Hearts £30,000 for Mackay in 1958, he was handing over a British record fee for a wing-half. Never was money more well-spent.

He was glad of his three Cup winner's medals in 1960, 1961 and 1967, for Mackay had a couple of nasty experiences at Wembley. As a schoolboy he was in a Scotland side thrashed 8-0 by a Johnny Haynes-inspired England.

Scotland the Brave might have been Mackay's battle-hymn, so it requires little imagination to guess his feelings at being beaten 9-3 by England in 1961.

In 1968, Nicholson and Mackay came to the conclusion it was time to part. The old thundering up and down the field role was getting beyond Mackay. So Brian Clough dashed down the motorway, talked to Mackay for seven hours, and persuaded him that by playing in the back four and skippering the side he could lift Derby, who had finished 18th the season before, out of the Second Division.

He did just that, and the season after Mackay had left Derby for Swindon where he became player-manager, Derby used the foundations that Mackay's tutelage had laid to win the First Division title.

Mackay played his last football for Swindon. He became manager of Forest, moved on to Derby to succeed Clough and win another First Division Championship, and later joined Walsall as boss.

Be careful before you say that it has never been done in football. Check with Dave Mackay first.

Wilf Mannion

England, Middlesbrough, Hull City

Probably the best England forward lines of my time included Stan Matthews, Raich Carter, Tommy Lawton and Wilf Mannion.

Mannion was the smallest of the quartet in stature, but well able to compare with them in ability.

He would be a left-sided midfield player today and an almost guaranteed success, for he had the vision and wit to make oceans of space for himself.

Mannion could dribble if he had to, but got most satisfaction from taking defenders out of the game with shrewd passes. Lawton owes more than the odd England goal to a Mannion through-ball that has split a defence.

He reached his peak in May, 1947, giving a virtuoso performance in a Great Britain side which beat the Rest of Europe 6-1 at Hampden Park. He scored twice and drove the best defenders in Europe to utter distraction.

A Tees-sider to the core, Wilf Mannion was born close to Middlesbrough and played for the town club for all but the last 16 matches of his League career.

He was, by all accounts, a fine player in his schooldays, and it was a simple, natural progression when Middlesbrough signed him as a professional in September, 1936.

Less than a year later, and while still 17 years old, Wilf had begun his career in the First Division, developing the skills that were to delight so many in later days.

My great memories of Mannion are of watching this brilliant inside-forward link with Raich Carter soon after the war, and marvelling at the way they could complement each other.

Wilf was blond and striking. A short man, only 5ft 5in tall, he was nevertheless uniformly sturdy and strong. He scored fewer goals than Carter, but was truly incomparable in a role that would now be called schemer. Close control and accuracy

Wilf Mannion of Middlesbrough and England, one of the last in a great tradition of scheming inside-forwards.

in the pass were his hallmarks.

He had played little more than 60 League games when the war interrupted his progress, and although he made his first England appearance in a wartime international, his drafting to the Middle East in 1943 could, it was feared, stunt his career.

Instead, he returned immediately to the England side for the first peace-time international and scored three goals in the 7-2 thrashing of Ireland in Belfast. Wilf played eight England games that season, scoring seven times. His stock had never been higher. But, in 1948, he threatened his entire future by taking a stand on an internal issue and refusing to re-sign for his club.

For a while, he went so far as to take another job – outside the game. But after losing a good deal in wages, and his England place, he relented and returned.

It did not take Mannion long to regain his position in the national side and he kept it until 1951. Wilf, by then, was into his thirties and perhaps no longer the power that he had been immediately after the war.

Mannion and Middlesbrough finally parted company in 1954, by which time he had played almost 350 League games and scored 99 goals.

His affair with Hull was brief. He flirted with a managerial job at Cambridge, but failed to hold it. Finally, Wilf Mannion went back to Tees-side and worked on a building site. It was a sad postscript to the career of one of England's greatest inside-forwards.

Josef Masopust

Czechoslovakia, Union Teplice,
Dukla Prague, Crossing

In 1962 the Continental sports writers bestowed their highest accolade on Josef

Masopust. They made him European Footballer of the Year, and though I do not claim to have inside knowledge of what influenced their voting decisions, I suspect that Masopust succeeded because of his outstanding performaces for Czechoslavakia in the World Cup series in Chile.

His attacking flair was an important factor in the Czechs reaching their first World Cup Final since 1934 when they were beaten in the last stage by the host nation, Italy.

On this occasion the Czechs' opponents were no less formidable – Brazil, playing in their own continent, though in the Santiago stadium.

The Czechs began with something of a bonus because the Brazilians decided not to risk Pelé who had not recovered from an injury which kept him out of the three previous matches.

Czechoslovakia proceeded to capitalise on it in the best possible manner – with a goal in the first quarter of an hour, and what a spendidly conceived effort it proved.

Scherer and Pospichal caught the defence in a momentary state of uncertainty and before the Brazilians could regroup, the ever-vigilant Masopust had burst into the penalty area. He timed his run so perfectly that he was able to meet the expected through pass and crash the ball past Gylmar. Within two minutes Brazil had equalised and though Masopust continued to dominate the midfield with his brilliant attacking probes, the Czechs gradually lost their poise.

Still they stayed in contention until the final 20 minutes or so when the Brazilians added two further goals to win the match and the Jules Rimet trophy by 3-1.

I always consider that the goal which Masopust scored in that World Cup Final typified his calm, authoritative approach to all major games. His was the type of tempera-

Perhaps the best-known Czechoslovakian footballer was Josef Masopust, European Footballer of the Year, 1962.

ment which lifts the star performer above the rest.

Masopust was first capped in 1954 and altogether he made 63 international appearances before ending his career playing in Belgium.

Certainly I prefer to remember Masopust at the height of his powers rather than that sadder occasion for him in Bratislava in May, 1963, when he captained his country against England and was called off just before half-time. England won that match 4-2–and the Czechs were roundly booed by their own vociferous supporters. Memories are short indeed in international sport!

Stanley Matthews

England, Stoke City, Blackpool, Stoke City

For years football tried to unravel the secret of how the biggest name in the game did it, the way he mesmerised opponents. Nobody ever really succeeded.

Stanley Matthews was the marvel of his time, and that time in first-class football lasted 33 seasons from 1932 until he played his last Football League at the age of 50. On the way he collected a knighthood in 1965 for services to football, an OBE in 1957 and more adulation than has ever come the way of any other British footballer.

He was more than a footballer. He was a legend. He could fill grounds just by turning up to play. Even in his later years when he was nowhere near as effective as he was at his best, opposing teams would not dare to leave him unattended.

Matthews was also the first of the British professionals to realise his own commercial potential and exploit it. But it is his football we are more concerned about.

At his peak, from the late 1930s to the early 1950s, managers strove to find tactical ways to limit the mayhem and panic he was capable of creating, and they seldom succeeded.

The pre-war Stanley Matthews, unrecognisable, except in style, from the veteran maestro of the 1953 Cup Final.

There was many a left-back who fancied his chances of putting Matthews in his place. When they occasionally succeeded Matthews would forsake his beat along the right touchline and switch his tormenting to the inside-left position. The only way to be certain of stopping him was to prevent him getting the ball. Once he got it nobody knew when they were going to get it back.

For a dribbling player he was very direct. Almost predictable. He would take the ball up to the full-back, beat him, go down the touchline beating any other opponent who came across to take him, until he got to the goal-line. Then he would pull back a pin-point cross that would either curl away from the goalkeeper and fall just beyond his reach, or roll diagonally towards the edge of the penalty area straight into the path of an on-coming striker.

Everybody knew what was going to happen. But stopping it ... that was different.

Apart from his early days, he was very much just a maker of goals for others. It is futile to ask why he failed to score more. It was just not his way. He was his own man.

He played 54 peace-time games for

127

Stanley Matthews goes down the right wing with a defender, as usual, straining in pursuit, in this case Curtis of Newcastle.

England plus another 26 during the war. The first was in September, 1934, and the last in April, 1957, when he was past his 42nd birthday.

He also starred in the most dramatic FA Cup final, always referred to as the Matthews Final, in 1953 when Blackpool beat Bolton 4-3. Matthews had been on the losing side with Blackpool in the finals of 1948 and 1951. He was then 38, and it was going to be his last chance of getting a winner's medal.

With 20 minutes to go Blackpool were 3-1 down. Then came the fairy-tale ending. Matthews made a goal for Stan Mortensen to make it 3-2. With two minutes to go Mortensen slammed home a free-kick to make it 3-3. And in the last minute Matthews jinked through the Bolton defence to lay on the winner for winger Bill Perry. The nation went to sleep happy that night.

If that was the peak, the foothills were back in the Potteries in the 1920s where Jack Matthews, 'The Fighting Barber of Hanley', made sure that his three sons, including Stanley, were doing their deep-breathing exercises by the open window at six o'clock in the morning.

This spartan start to life was one of Matthews' secrets. He never drank, never smoked, never stopped training. And he was still playing in retirement in Malta in the middle 1970s.

The schoolboy prodigy was an office-boy at Stoke City when he was 15, and doing the two miles between his Hanley home and the Victoria Grounds on foot, for fitness. On his 17th birthday he signed professional and made his debut in March, 1932.

At 18 he was a first-team regular in Stoke's promotion-winning Second Division side. At 19 he was an England player. The curtain was up. The longest individual soccer show of them all was on the road.

Off the field Matthews melted into the

background. Quiet, polite, with no flamboyance, he nevertheless knew his own worth. In 1937 he asked for a transfer. The Potteries stopped. Three thousand attended a public meeting and there was another thousand outside. The placards shouted that Matthews should not go. He didn't.

War broke out. He joined the RAF and spent most of his time stationed near Blackpool as a physical training instructor. After the war he went back to Stoke, even though he had acquired a hotel at the Lancashire resort.

Following an injury he was asked to play in Stoke's reserve team to prove his fitness. The manager did not want to disturb a winning side.

Matthews refused, forced the issue, and was transferred in 1947 to Blackpool for £11,000. For that sum they were to get 14 years of crowd-pulling Matthews, three FA Cup finals and the best, most successful, years in their history.

The legend became the first Footballer of the Year in 1948. As late as 1955 he was still in the England team, making five of the goals when England beat Scotland 7-2 at Wembley.

By 1961, even the ageless Matthews was finding the First Division more exacting and his relationship with Blackpool was not what it had been.

Stoke's young manager Tony Waddington, his team flailing about at the foot of the Second Division, had the brilliant vision of bringing the maestro back to the Potteries.

He coughed up £2,500 and, amid unprecedented fervour, Matthews was back home. The following season, 1962-63, borne on the floodtide of euphoria and a few other shrewd signings, Stoke chased promotion. From the last match of the season, Stoke needed a point to ensure going up. They were one up at half-time. Obviously they badly needed another. They got it—from Matthews, the last goal of his career! Stan always had a sense of the dramatic.

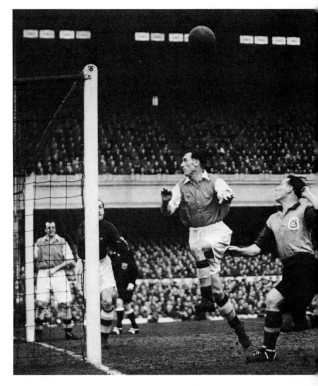

Joe Mercer, in his Arsenal days, heads away as Iggleden of Leeds closes in.

Joe Mercer

England, Everton, Arsenal

Surely there can never have been a more optimistic player than Joe Mercer, an inspiring, attacking left-half who changed his game to suit the circumstances of injury. As a captain, and he led England's wartime teams many times, he must have been one of the best. He had the gift of making people play for him.

Perhaps because he always believed that it was a game to be enjoyed, he always played it with a smile on his face. He did have advantages. He was on the winning side more than most.

He pretends to never having been much of a player. But he comes of League football stock—his father played for Forest—and he always had the wit to play it intelligently and within his limitations.

129

Mercer could beat his man when he had to, but his game was based on winning the ball and then knocking it out quickly. He was a master of the art of counter-attack.

Few people have been written off so many times as Joe was. The war might have finished him; Everton most certainly thought so. Then Arsenal bought him, thinking only in terms of a short-term investment. They had all reckoned without the lion-hearted spirit they were dealing with.

Joe grew up in the Wirral and played in the same Cheshire schoolboys side as Stan Cullis. Everton spotted him and signed him on professional forms when he reached 17. He was earning £5 a week!

He made his debut in the highly-talented Everton side of 1932-33, but it was his only game for two seasons. By 1935, he was virtually established. Oddly, because he was an adventurer at the time and loved to storm upfield with his forwards, Mercer scored his only goal for Everton in the 1935-36 season.

In the year before war broke out, Everton won the League Championship and Mercer was picked five times as left-half for England. Clearly, this light (11 stone) but immensely strong half-back with remarkably bent legs, was set for a decade at the top. Instead, his career was savaged, and even the 22 wartime internationals he was able to play could offer no real compensation.

Joe never played again for England, and 1946 brought the biggest crisis of his career. His knee was damaged in one of the final wartime internationals, and even an operation to remove the cartilage could not save him from a good deal of suffering.

Everton dropped him. At 31, with a bad knee and suspect legs anyway, they considered him a spent force. Arsenal, their own pride dismantled by the war and at its lowest ebb for 20 years, bought him for £7,000.

Joe was made club captain at Highbury in the hope that he would spend 'his last two or three years' repairing Arsenal's spirit as they built a new team. Mercer was to do very much more than that.

In 1948, Arsenal won the League Championship. Five years later they won it again – and Joe Mercer was still captain. Between the two titles, they reached the FA Cup final twice, beating Liverpool in 1950 and losing to Newcastle in 1952.

So what was the secret of eternal youth that Mercer seemed to have discovered? Or maybe it was discovered by Arsenal manager Tom Whittaker. Aiming to keep Mercer as long as possible – but never dreaming the truth – Whittaker played Mercer as a defensive wing-half, setting up attacks without joining them in his favourite fashion. Joe, I am sure, needed to discipline his natural energies to adjust. But adjust he did – and Arsenal had eight years of benefit.

When Arsenal won the Championship in 1953, the crowd massed on the Highbury pitch and chanted for Mercer to speak. Perhaps overcome with emotion, Mercer called it 'the most splendid day of my life' and promptly announced that he was retiring.

He did not, but perhaps he should have. For as the 1953-54 season neared its end, Mercer, now almost 40 years old, broke his left leg. Highbury hushed as he was loaded onto a stretcher, then stood and cheered. It was the end, and everyone knew it.

Joe, of course, did not say goodbye to football quite like that. He managed Sheffield United, Aston Villa and Manchester City, recovering from a stroke along the way, before arriving at my own Coventry City club first as general manager and then as a director.

Billy Meredith

Wales, Northwich Victoria,
Manchester City, Manchester United,
Manchester City

One of the happier aspects of the present-day game is the increasing emphasis which

Billy Meredith (left) playing for Manchester United against Queens Park Rangers in 1908.

clubs are putting on wing play, for surely there are few more exciting sights or, in fact, effective tactics, than a winger in full flight down the touchline.

In those halcyon days at the turn of the century there emerged one of the greatest of this type of forward – Billy Meredith who, with Stanley Matthews and Tom Finney, must rank as supreme craftsmen of their kind. Even before I began to interest myself in the unfolding story of Association Football, I had heard of Meredith's fame. Like Matthews, he won world renown both for his skill and longevity. He was just four months short of his 50th birthday when he played for Manchester City against Newcastle United in an FA Cup semi-final

in March, 1924, and he was almost 46 when he made his final appearance for Wales – against England at Highbury in March, 1920. Both these records still stand, a lasting testimony to a player who dedicated himself to fitness.

A playing career which spread from 1893 to 1924 started with Northwich Victoria, but in October, 1894, he moved to Manchester City and remained with them until 1906. In that year an investigation by the Football Association resulted in findings of illegal payments. Those players involved were told they could not remain with City and in the hiatus which followed Meredith decided to join neighbours Manchester United, where he gained FA Cup and League Championship honours.

He rejoined City in 1921 and remained with them until his retirement in 1924 by which time he had played in 682 League games.

Billy Meredith was both a creator and scorer of goals. Few showed more masterly control in dribbling to the corner flag and crossing the ball at just the right moment to onrushing colleagues. He was also adept at cutting inside the full-back and shooting with a precision which brought him 181 League goals with the two Manchester clubs. One goal which gave him particular pleasure was that which defeated Lancashire rivals, Bolton Wanderers, 1-0 in the 1904 FA Cup final at the original Crystal Palace.

Until recent times, when Ivor Allchurch and Cliff Jones overtook him, Meredith held the record for the number of Welsh caps, 48, an astonishing total when one remembers that all of them were gained in the Home International Championship. In those far-off days, of course, there were no matches against foreign opposition for Welsh teams.

He made his debut in a 2-2 draw against Northern Ireland in Belfast on March 16, 1895, and closed his international career in that farewell match in London exactly a quarter of a century later. And what a marvellous finale it proved as Wales achieved one of their rare victories on English soil by a 2-1 margin.

During 30 years as a player Meredith took part in more than 1,000 matches and received £1,580 from various benefit matches staged on his behalf in 1913. No wonder he was dubbed 'The Prince of Wingers'!

Bobby Moore

England, West Ham United, Fulham

I imagine that Bobby Moore's retirement might have taken some people by surprise. They could be forgiven for thinking he would go on for ever, so easy did he make the game look.

I think he would have been a magnificent poker player, especially if he were playing with the richest of gamblers, because his outstanding attribute was that the higher you raised the stakes in terms of world competition the higher he was able to raise his game.

At times, down at Upton Park, West Ham fans must have thought he was not in top gear but that was because of his economical way of playing the game. Not many opponents would agree with a claim of lack of commitment.

The truth was that while others had to rush about to be effective, Bobby, as the consequence of his fantastic football brain, was able to defend successfully while moving only the minimum number of yards.

Yet when he was stretched in world competition against players like Pelé and Eusebio we were able to see defensive football at its very highest level.

Bobby seemed to be able to read a pass before the idea occurred in the mind of the opponent and that was his secret weapon.

I have mentioned his defensive qualities, because when a man plays in a deep position with a No. 6 on his back, those have to be his first responsibilities, but maybe that is doing an injustice to Bobby's capabilities when he was in possession of the ball.

He was such an accurate passer, long range or short, and with either foot, that other players must have despaired of emulating him.

Bobby was so easy to play with. He gave the ball where an opponent found it hardest to tackle the receiver, and was always in command of the situation. Bobby did not explode the ball at people like a firework but eased it gently to them in such a way that their next move was simplified.

I have heard so-called knowledgeable people say that Bobby tackled like a wet lettuce. Having been on the end of a Moore tackle I can assure you that it was anything but a pleasant experience.

Bobby always tackled his weight. He

Near-post vigilance of Bobby Moore, holder of a record 108 England caps.

132

always sought to let the opponent know he was still there, and although he never went out of his way to mix it, he could take care of himself in tight corners if necessary.

As a captain he operated more by example than by inspiration or shouting in the heat of battle. His very coolness gave the impression to his colleagues that everything was all right, and although the other team were entitled to be on the field with them, there was no way they were going to cause Bobby to rush about or disturb his elegant approach.

It was that superior, calm manner that rubbed off to England's advantage in those great days of 1966 when we won the World Cup.

To those outside the capital, Bobby has always been the epitome of a Londoner. To Londoners themselves, he is an East-ender. Born in Barking in 1941, and schooled in Leyton, he reached school-leaving age quite uncertain of his future.

Although it seems odd, no football club had approached him. 'All my mates had gone off for trials with different clubs,' he relates. 'But nobody seemed to want me.'

Belatedly, West Ham stepped in to make perhaps their most significant signing ever. Bobby was soon on his way, winning the first of a record 18 England Youth caps, then signing professional in June, 1958.

Things then began to happen at a speed which must surely have damaged a man of less maturity. Even at this early age, Bobby was single-minded in his ambitions, and nobody's fool in the high-finance world in which he was rapidly involving himself.

He made his League debut against Manchester United at 17, and won the first of eight Under-23 caps two years later. In 1962, when just 21, he was named in England's World Cup squad and collected the first of his 108 full caps in the warm-up game against Peru.

Bobby's England career began in the No. 4 shirt and he retained it for the four World Cup matches, including the defeat against

Brazil which began the massive mutual respect between Bobby and Pelé.

When he became the youngest-ever captain of England, leading his country against Czechoslovakia in May of 1963, the image of the rich, blond and handsome star was already close to completion.

Now, however, he sought success at club level – a success that West Ham, for all the public affection they commanded, had never threatened to supply. Tottenham, wallowing in their own golden age, were

rumoured to be prepared to bid, but the conjecture was stifled by a change for the better at Upton Park.

The friendly no-hopers turned into aristocratic winners. They took the FA Cup in 1964, days after Bobby had been named Footballer of the Year. The following season, they enchanted 100,000 at Wembley by defeating Munich 1860 2-0 to carry off the European Cup-Winners Cup. That triumph also ensured they would retain their most precious property.

Bobby Moore, seen playing for West Ham against Crystal Palace, brought a new glamorous image to British footballers.

The face of Bobby Moore became the face of football, emblazoned on adverts for hair-cream and gravy. He became a business success, guiding his own company with a shrewdness born of an upbringing in the cut and thrust toughness of the East End.

It was as if the 1966 World Cup had been laid on for Bobby. England were host country; the world was to be his stage for a fortnight. Then, three months before the finals, he slapped in another transfer request which was refused.

He got over it, of course, and the rumours that Sir Alf Ramsey would discard him proved unfounded. He was at his peak through the series; his plans operated faultlessly. The image he had long had of himself lifting the Cup was played out in reality.

If anything, he took more criticism for his triumphs. The carpers began to make innuendos about his life-style, which was certainly and understandably that of a very wealthy man. Bob never once seemed concerned, however, and his composure passed the ultimate test during the sordid episode in Bogota before the 1970 World Cup, when he was arrested on the laughable charge of stealing a bracelet.

The most appropriate comment on it all came from Alan Mullery: 'Steal a bracelet? With Bobby's money, he could have bought the shop!' The judge agreed, Moore rejoined the England side in Mexico City and played assuredly throughout the tournament to earn Pelé's accolade as 'The finest defender in the world'. Nevertheless, he still suffered the heartbreak of World Cup dismissal at the quarter-final stage, England having led West Germany by two goals.

A more realistic slur on his career was the incident in November of 1970, when he and three other West Ham players were seen drinking in a night-club on the eve of a Cup-tie at Blackpool. West Ham lost 4-0, Bobby played uncharacteristically badly and was disciplined with a fine and being dropped for five weeks.

He came back as if nothing had happened. Ramsey restored him to the England side and he completed his international career against Italy in 1973. The following year he ended his 18-year association with West Ham, joined Fulham and proved that nothing was beyond the realms of fairy-tales by guiding them to the 1975 FA Cup final . . . against West Ham.

Alan Morton

Scotland, Queen's Park, Glasgow Rangers

Alan Morton, the tiny, darting genius whom his admirers affectionately called the 'Wee Blue Devil', tantalised and tormented defences between the two world wars, none more so than England's. Scottish supporters of long memory and those whose task it is to recreate memorabilia for a new generation of football enthusiasts, will probably point to one match above the rest which epitomises Morton's magical qualities on the left wing. That was the 1928 Home International Championship fixture at Wembley when a diminutive Scottish forward line, in which Alec Jackson at 5ft 7in, was easily the tallest, outclassed England and gave their country a magnificent victory by five goals to one. Jackson scored a hat-trick and Alex James got the two other goals, but much of the build-up moves were fashioned and inspired by the 5ft 4in Morton. The manner in which Morton destroyed defences brought him hero-worship from Scottish fans. A swerve of the body could leave a full-back stranded; a moment of pure dribbling skill carved an opening where none existed, and his floating crosses almost carried the message 'goal', so accurately were they judged.

The application which Morton used to perfect his game provides an example to all who seek glory in the sporting arena. He practised assiduously in the essential arts of control and balance; thus his tiny frame was never a handicap, although he took his share of buffetings from opponents who knew no other way of trying to stop him.

Cold statistics inform us that between 1913 and 1933 he made 565 League appearances and won 31 caps, nine League Championship medals and two Cup winners' medals – an array of achievement which underlines his consistent performances throughout the 1920s.

Queen's Park gave him his early chances and he stayed seven years with them before signing for Rangers in 1920, playing in 379 League games while his club took the League title with monotonous regularity.

While the 'Wembley Wizards' victory must stand out as the highspot of Morton's international career, there were many other satisfying occasions, including a 3-1 success over France in Paris on May 8, 1932. That happened to be both his first international against overseas opposition *and* his final game for Scotland.

That wayward genius Hughie Gallacher, another member of that great Wembley side, enjoyed many a scoring field-day when Morton was operating his special brand of football alchemy on the left flank. Once he scored four times against the Irish in Belfast and when asked to comment on the feat, told his interviewer: 'It's the wee fella y'know . . . he lays them on' . . . and Hughie stood only 5ft 6in himself!

Perhaps, having noted the personal performances and contributions which Alan Morton made to Scottish football, you will not be entirely surprised to learn that he was also the highest paid player of his era, at least north of the border.

Alan Morton, the original 'Wee Blue Devil' and scourge of the English.

Gerd Muller

West Germany, Bayern Munich

Anybody built less like a goalscorer than Gerd Muller it would be impossible to imagine. He defies all the concepts of what a lithe marksman must have going for him. Unfortunately for all the theorists, he spent a lifetime defying goalkeepers and centre-halves.

All the pictures show the unique Muller shape. The legs should belong somewhere else. They are fantastic. It seems only a slight exaggeration to suggest that they are as wide as they are long.

But those calf muscles are like footballs. Muller is well below average height. But the legs allowed him to take off from the ground and get to balls in the air when it seemed obvious to everybody that he had absolutely no chance of reaching them.

They also gave him the terrific strength to be able to withstand the strongest of tackles and turn quickly in the penalty area. And they are almost entirely the reason for the tremendous power Muller got behind his shots.

With legs like that he should have been slow. He was anything but. He was far sharper than the average striker.

His ability to get goals was rivalled only by Jimmy Greaves. But there the similarity ended. Jimmy finessed most of his in. Muller exploded his, and throughout his long career, West Germany's scoring hero averaged nearly a goal a match. In fairness to Greaves, I should say that there are weaker defences towards the bottom of the Bundesliga than in the English First Division.

Muller also made the fullest use of a powerful backside. When Muller shrugged players off they stayed shrugged! And when defenders charged him, it was like hitting a lump of rock.

'The King of the Penalty Box' will be remembered longest by England fans for the goal he crashed past Peter Bonetti at Leon to knock Alf Ramsey's men out of the 1970 World Cup in the quarter-final. It helped to make him the tournament's leading scorer with ten goals.

That should have startled nobody. Muller banged in 33 goals in his first 29 international matches, a stupendous striking rate at that level. Twice he was West Germany's Footballer of the Year. He has also been European Footballer of the Year.

He would have to scratch his Bavarian head to remember his best goal, but perhaps his most significant was the winner he got to make West Germany World Champions again when they conquered Holland 2-1 in the 1974 final in Munich.

Forty-six goals in two seasons of junior football enticed the scouts of several leading German clubs, but Bayern pounced faster than the others and in the summer of 1963 Muller was a Munich man.

Twelve months later Bayern won pro-

Left **Gerd Muller (West Germany) and Wim Rijsbergen (Holland) in a heading duel.**

The ace marksman Gerd Muller who averaged over a goal a match for West Germany.

motion to the Bundesliga. Muller's 35 goals might have had some bearing on their success! The following season was not good enough by Muller standards. He scored only 14 goals, but Bayern managed to win the West German Cup.

By October, 1966, Muller had forced his way into the German national team, being remodelled after losing the World Cup final to England a few months earlier.

Now there was no holding Muller. In 1966-67, when he was still only 21, he scored 47 goals and helped Bayern take the Cup Winner's Cup and the German Cup. He beat Franz Beckenbauer, no less, to the Footballer of the Year award by 417 votes to 60.

From then on, it was success all the way. He became the most feared striker in the world, but retained all his natural modesty.

Again, like Greaves, he has said that he does not know how he scores goals. The magic is beyond self-analysis. It never worried Muller, who was a most amiable character. A better business sense would undoubtedly have made him more money. But then he would not have been the engaging fellow he became.

Somebody once suggested that had he been more single-minded he could have scored even more goals. The man who made that suggestion was not a goalkeeper. Goalkeepers knew their Muller, a man who retired from international football with the mind-bending figures of 68 goals in 62 matches.

Igor Netto

Russia, Spartak Moscow

Grace and artistry are not words one automatically associates with footballers from the USSR but they fit perfectly Igor Netto, who for more than 20 years delighted football purists far beyond the confines of his own country.

He won 56 caps and the total would have been far greater had not injury disrupted his career at important stages, not least when he was limited to a single match during the 1958 World Cup final rounds in Sweden.

With his fair hair and supple movements Igor could scarcely remain unobtrusive, and once attention had settled on him it was often difficult to look elsewhere. There was a strength and purpose about all his play. When danger threatened, this industrious half-back would frequently take the heat off with a sharp tackle and thoughtful clearance. In attacking situations he was never far from his forwards and I thought he excelled when leading Russia in the 1962 World Cup series in Chile, quietly inspiring his colleagues by his own efficient example. Previously he had captained Russia when they won the Melbourne Olympics of 1956.

Obviously he stands alongside such Russian giants as Valentin Ivanov and Lev Yashin, that goalkeeper extraordinary of neighbours Dynamo, and his record for Spartak eloquently expresses his consistency in the domestic game in the USSR.

He made 367 league appearances in 14 seasons during which time he won five Championship medals and three Cup-winners' medals.

There was universal delight throughout his country when in 1957 he was awarded the Order of Lenin, the Soviet Union's most prized honour.

In his latter years as a player Igor moved to centre back where he was able to save his legs while using his head wisely to control the middle of the defence. The switch gave his play an extra dimension. Younger colleagues learned to feed off his shrewdly dispatched passes and in 1965 he was re-called to the national side at the age of 35.

If he were to choose one of his memorable matches I dare say Igor might select the European Nations Cup final held in Paris in July, 1960. He led the Russians to a thrilling 2-1 victory over Yugoslavia after the game had gone into extra time. And he will not mind being reminded in this context that he scored the Yugoslavs' goal!

Honoured Master of Sport Igor Netto, the day Russia won the European Nations Cup in 1960.

The last of the great attacking centre-halves, Ernst Ocwirk of Austria, in 1950.

The last I heard of Igor was that he was actively involved in coaching. If he was able to translate his own high skills to a rising generation of Russian footballers, the redoubtable Igor may well see some of his protégés in the 1980 Olympics in Moscow.

Ernst Ocwirk

Austria, Stalau, FAC Vienna, FK Austria, Sampdoria

In recent years Austrian football has lived very much in the shadows of that of neighbours West Germany, but that was not the case when Ernst Ocwirk bestrode the centre of his country's defence in the early 1950s.

I suppose he was probably very near the height of his powers when he skippered Austria to third place in the 1954 World Cup in Switzerland. The Austrians beat Scotland

1-0 and then thrashed Czechoslovakia 5-0 in their other group game. In the quarter final they took part in a remarkably high-scoring match against Switzerland which they finally won 7-5, Ocwirk scoring one of his team's goals.

Yet but for the Austrians deciding to withdraw from the 1950 World Cup finals in Brazil, Ocwirk would certainly have made his mark at the highest level of the game far earlier.

He had, in fact, played first for his country in 1947 and was in the Austrian Olympic team which played in London the following year.

In physique, as in tactical approach, Ocwirk was a commanding figure. He was tall and magnificently built for the job he did with such clinical expertise, first at centre-half, then at wing-half and then as a deep-

141

lying inside-forward when he ventured into Italian football with Sampdoria of Genoa.

His admirers in Britain dubbed him 'Clockwork' which was as much a tribute to his consistency as it was a play on his surname.

He was born in Vienna in 1926 and joined FK Austria after playing for Stalau and FAC Vienna. While he was with FK they won the Austrian League championship four times, in 1949, 1950, 1953 and 1962 — and in the 1949 and 1962 seasons the club also won the domestic Cup competition.

Many British followers will remember Ocwirk when he captained the Rest of the World team which drew a match of intense drama with England 4-4 at Wembley in October, 1953, Alf Ramsey saving the host nation's face with a penalty in the last 25 seconds. He organised the cosmopolitan talents of half a dozen countries with such skill that the world team quickly knitted into a smooth working unit. Indeed, long before the end it would have been difficult for the uninitiated to differentiate between the scratch side and the established combination.

Ocwirk represented his country in 62 internationals and after he retired as a player, he accepted coaching appointments in Italy, Germany and his homeland.

Pelé

Brazil, Santos, New York Cosmos

Pelé was the outstanding player in the world for many years. To qualify that bald understatement I need to add that Pelé was outstanding for many reasons, not the least important being his influence on the game as a whole from the moment when he came into World Cup football in Sweden in 1958.

Pelé was 17 then, and he cried his eyes out for Brazil's victory. Humility was always one of the great man's strong points. He once said: 'I am not proud that I can sometimes make goals out of nothing. It makes me humble because it is a talent that God gave me. All I can do is use it well.'

Pelé did. He won World Cup winners' medals in 1958 and 1970, and would have done so in Chile in 1962 had he not been injured. He made more than 100 appearances for Brazil and scored more than 100 goals for his country. For himself, and that includes Brazil and his club Santos, he scored more than 1,000 goals. He caused everybody who saw him play to envy talents that are virtually beyond description. Even if he had never done all that, he would go down in soccer history as the man who did more than anybody else to sell—perhaps project is a better word—the game to the United States.

When America finally stages the finals of the World Cup they should get Pelé to open the tournament. After what he has done for the game, he deserves nothing less.

What made Pelé the player he was? First, his physique was perfect for football. He had a magnificent frame in which every muscle was superbly developed. He possessed speed to burn, and balance that a Swiss watchmaker could not have improved upon.

If that is not enough, then he had the arts and crafts of the game in a greater measure than any other player anybody has ever seen.

He combined effectiveness with great beauty and style. Just to see him, for one fleeting moment, take a ball on his chest was to observe athleticism of the highest standard, well worth the admission money on its own. No other player could ever do it quite as well. When Pelé was taking the ball in the air his touch achieved the same peak of perfection as when he was taking it on the ground.

He had power and accuracy when it came to shooting, and he cared little which foot he used.

He also had to cultivate, and I intend no unkindness, a little bit of nastiness without

Pelé leaps for a header with an Italian defender during the World Cup Final of 1970.

which he would not have survived. Through the years, legions of players have been sent out with instructions to kick him out of the game. He had to have a few weapons in his own armoury to protect him against that, and so would anyone else.

I think the development of that outlook helped to make him an even better player, because unless the game degenerated into total brutality nobody could really kick him out of the match. Pelé was always going to wait his moment and show the offender, with the help of a bruise or two, that Pelé was playing.

Apart from that aspect, unfortunately forced upon him, Pelé was to be congratulated on his temperament. For the football playing itself, he was marvellously relaxed. Also, for all those off-the-field activities involved in promoting the game, especially to youngsters, he showed a remarkable amount of patience, even allowing that he was being paid well for it.

He will always be remembered for his influence off the field as well as for what he achieved on it. To have achieved so much, and for so long, is really the epitaph to Pelé's playing career.

Former Brazil team-manager Joao Saldanha once said: 'Pelé is to Brazilian football what Shakespeare is to English literature.'

Even Pelé, or Edson Arantes do Nascimento, as it says on his birth certificate, had to have a Stratford upon Avon. It was at Tres Coracoes, roughly translated into Three Hearts, and it will shock nobody to be told that there is now a statue of Pelé there.

The Santos club of Sao Paulo found and kept him. In the end they were demanding such high guarantees for tour matches that I think Pelé was keeping them!

He hit the Brazilian headlines first in 1957 when he scored eight goals in one game. A

The best player in the world, Pelé, near the end of his days with Santos in 1973.

cap against Argentina followed, and the rest is well-known history.

It is barely possible to imagine a better player than the incomparable Edson. Why should we try? If someone else wants to be regarded as better than Pelé, then let him try and earn it.

Jesse Pennington

England, West Bromwich Albion

Perhaps Jesse Pennington's chief claim to fame, and it is one he would have liked, is having his name tossed into the ring every time a Black Country soccer fan is asked to illustrate his favourite example of sportsmanship.

Pennington's beloved Albion – his father helped to found the club – had never won the FA Cup with Pennington in the side. They were playing Barnsley in a replay of the final at Bramall Lane, Sheffield, in 1912. In the last minute, with the game still goal-less as in the first match, a Barnsley player was streaking through with the goal at his mercy. Pennington could have brought him down by conceding a penalty. He did not, and Albion lost the Cup.

Pennington would not have wanted to know about the professional foul, even if the phrase had been invented then. It just would not have been right for a man who was proud of being Albion's captain and proud of his 25 England caps, most of them won during his famous full-back partnership with Bob Crompton, of Blackburn Rovers.

Pennington, who played on the left, was deft where Crompton was doughty. It made no difference. They complemented each other perfectly. The Albion man was light of frame and took the ball delicately. He tended to stroke it about where Crompton was more emphatic.

His style and positional skill served Pennington well. A career that lasted 18 years began in 1903-04. When it finished he was 38 but Anno Domini had not stopped him playing in 37 First Division games and

Jesse Pennington was a great full-back whose name has become associated with sportsmanship.

earning his last two England caps two seasons earlier when West Bromwich won the League Championship for the only time.

It was not a question of Pennington staying loyal to one club throughout his career. He would have regarded the thought of leaving Albion as sacrilege. He played in 455 League games, winning a Second Division Championship medal in 1910-11, and laid down a standard for left-back play which many tried to copy but few achieved.

Ferenc Puskas

Hungary, Spain, Honved, Real Madrid

'The Galloping Major', captain of the Hungarian team which shattered England's thin veil of invincibility at Wembley in 1953, was playing for Europe against Great Britain in an ex-internationals' charity match at Leicester.

Above **The biggest disappointment of Puskas (right, shooting) was defeat by West Germany in the 1954 World Cup Final.**

Below **Ninety minutes away from England's biggest shock. Ferenc Puskas leads out the Hungarians who destroyed England's record in 1953.**

It was 20 years after Puskas' prime, the British team was a bit younger and it was expected to put Europe under pressure. Puskas was getting on a bit and the build, barely on the right side of being described as portly, suggested that old-style fireworks were out.

Instead, we all got a 90-minute lesson on how the game should be played.

If the ball were played anywhere near him, it was his; the control was instant and perfect. He was a master at screening the ball; players in twos and threes would ferret round him looking for a chance to sneak the ball away but I have seldom, if ever, seen a player use his body, despite the pot, so well.

The passes were beautifully accurate, and struck with perfection. The pace was judged to the inch to make it easier for his team-mates. Twenty years on and Puskas was proving that old dogs do not need to be taught new tricks.

But, back to 1953. Those who saw it will never forget the feint that stranded Billy Wright, the ball dragged back by the sole of the foot and then flicked round the bemused opponent.

Its significance lies in the fact that it proved that in some respects footballers can be made, because since Puskas demonstrated how it was done the coaches got to work, until almost every professional footballer could achieve a passable imitation of what was apparently unbelievable magic.

What power Puskas had in that left foot. It caused a lot of people to look upon him as one-footed. That was far from the case as his right was deadly accurate, too. But that left was so special that it must remain one of the most exceptional single weapons possessed by any player.

What impressed me about the Hungarians of 1953, and I was a professional footballer by then, remember, was their amazing vision, acquired through their planned training programme. They learned to control the ball perfectly while their heads were high in the air, assessing the movements of opponents and team-mates alike.

Their command of the ball was still precise, but their tactical appreciation and capacity to read a game raised it to a level that made so many other national sides look like novices alongside them.

Puskas was a king and commander in this tactical mastery. He was a general, but if he needed the pace and aggression of an infantryman, then he had that, too. He and his Hungarian colleagues revolutionised football thinking in Britain, and maybe the cornerstone of England's success in the 1966 World Cup was laid by the Hungarian national team playing a beautiful brand of football that I shall never forget.

Puskas says that the reason he developed all that skill with the left foot was because, coming from a very poor family, his father could afford only one pair of shoes between Puskas and one of his brothers. Puskas got the right one, and was too scared to hit a ball with it!

His outstanding ability got him into the Honved club at the age of 13. He played in his first international at 17, and was to hold his place in the team for 11 years until the national rising in 1956. He had scored 85 goals in 84 games when the troubles came. He was on tour with Honved and decided not to return home.

He settled in Austria for a year, and then went to Madrid to start a second startling career with Real at the age of 30.

Puskas, whose injury had probably cost Hungary the World Cup won by West Germany in 1954, became part of the finest club side that has ever been assembled. It included players from South America as well as Latin and Eastern European countries, and the partnership Puskas struck with Alfred di Stefano can hardly ever have been surpassed. The pair tortured every defence they played against.

Puskas, who still keeps his home in a magnificent villa just outside Madrid, amassed a huge amount of money during his playing days in Spain for whom he gained four caps. He lost a lot of it in business ventures he lacked the time to supervise, but eventually he had to stop playing.

Panathinaikos, then a rising force in Greece where there was no shortage of money for football, offered him the manager's job and he took it, and took them to the final of the European Cup which they lost 2-0 to Ajax at Wembley.

But whatever he could achieve as a manager was never likely to dim the memory of Puskas the player who scorned the celebrations when Pelé got his 1,000th goal. Puskas reckoned the Brazilian was at least 500 behind him!

Luigi Riva

Italy, Cagliari

Was Riva a centre-forward or was he a left-winger? Not even he himself could really make up his mind. But what he and everybody else knew was that when he set off on

A man whose shooting made the fans hold their breath, Luigi Riva of Cagliari and Italy.

one of those diagonal charges towards the penalty spot Italian crowds would hush in expectation.

They were waiting for one of the hardest shots to launch yet another missile. This is what they paid their money to come and see, and Riva was quite aware of his value. At his peak in the early 1970s he was taking around £51,000 a year from his club and doubling that income from sources outside the game.

In one way, Riva deserved every penny. He, more than anybody else, changed the face of Italian soccer from the dreadful defensive stuff that demoralised us all in the early and middle 1960s. He had the power and the stamina to keep taking on defences. Just as important, he had the courage, too.

Obviously, he took a lot of punishment

148

and, like Dave Mackay, twice came back from a broken leg.

Orphaned very early in life, Riva has always been able to look after himself in more ways than one. He has become a folk hero in Cagliari since moving there in 1963 when they were a Second Division side. Riva took them into the First Division on a tide of goals and did more than most to keep them there.

Italy used him first in 1965. He looked certain to come to England for the 1966 World Cup but did not. He was in Mexico in 1970 when Italy reached the final, and went to West Germany for the 1974 tournament.

In Mexico, he was the man they all feared. Italy, not the most prolific of scorers, had made the finals on the strength of no more than ten goals. Riva had got seven of them! Just before that he had taken Cagliari to their first Championship, too!

For that, the Sardinians were almost ready to give him their island. He repaid them in 1973 by deciding to stay when powerful Juventus were talking in terms of £1½ million for his signature.

Gianni Rivera

Italy, Alessandria, AC Milan

Rivera was the golden boy of Italian football almost as soon as he had made his debut for AC Milan in the early 1960s following a £130,000 transfer from Alessandria. By Italian standards there seems nothing remarkable about that sort of fee – except that Rivera was only 16 at the time.

Rivera was an inside-forward of superb skill and touch who had a mind very much of his own. His career was littered with the debris from brushes with authority, but in a perverse sort of way he had the last laugh when he gained control of Milan. Surely this was the ideal instance of the 'if you cannot beat them, join them' thinking.

Rivera, not much more than a boy then, played for AC Milan against Benfica in the 1963 European Cup final at Wembley, and it

The golden boy of Italian football, Gianni Rivera.

was immediately apparent that the world had acquired a new star.

The accuracy of his passing and his ability to find holes in a defence where none seemed to exist gave the game a different dimension to British eyes. Yet for all that skill, Rivera packed a pretty hefty shot, too.

He won virtually every honour except a World Cup winner's medal and four World Cups bear testimony to how hard he tried to achieve that.

Rivera achieved notoriety of a different kind when he battled with the Italian team manager who dropped him from the side during the 1970 finals in Mexico. Eventually the president of the Italian FA had to intervene. Rivera half won his battle. He played three times, twice as substitute.

Milan had won 2-1 at Wembley in Rivera's first European Cup final, with Rivera making both the goals. His influence on the team grew. Milan competed for European honours nearly every year. He was made captain for a time though eventually succeeded by the less volatile Giancinto Facchetti.

Controversy and headlines followed Rivera all the time, but the Italians flocked to see him, probably enjoying his clashes with the establishment.

However difficult he might have been in dressing-room politics, he must have been a beautiful player to have alongside.

Djalma Santos

Brazil, Portuguesa de Desportos, Palmeiras, Atletico Paranaense

I have always felt that Djalma Santos represented all that was best in Brazilian football. He knew extreme poverty as a child, yet as he acquired comparative wealth and fame, he remained a model of fairness, without a trace of that arrogance and pettiness which sometimes mars the character of world-class footballers who have risen from modest environs.

He was splendidly proportioned for a fullback and his composure in the most taut contest was a marvellous antidote to the theatrical and sometimes inflammatory attitudes of some colleagues. I well remember his calming influence in that unhappy quarter-final match between Brazil and Hungary at Berne during the 1954 World Cup series, particularly when he persuaded Julinho from precipitate action against the referee, Mr Arthur Ellis.

One of the many facets of Brazilian football which has appealed to me is the willingness of youngsters to learn the basic skills. There is an impression in Europe that you

Gianni Rivera playing in the 1970 World Cup. His winner against West Germany in extra time took Italy to the Final.

150

Djalma Santos (left) with two of his great Brazilian colleagues Zito and Pelé in 1963, the year after Brazil's second World Cup win.

need only toss a ball to a Brazilian boy and he will perform a repertoire of tricks. The real truth is that young Brazilians apply themselves from their formative years to practising control. Thus Djalma's frighteningly efficient lobs and penalty kicks were gifts he created by endless hours of training and not bestowed on him by nature.

Djalma, who came from Sao Paulo, first prospered with Portuguesa de Desportos between 1947 and 1958 and then spent ten years with Palmeiras. He remained with them, latterly as a youth team coach, until he was persuaded from retirement to play for Atletico Paranaense of Coritiba in the State of Parana. Incredibly, he was still playing at the age of 41, and altogether he appeared in more than 1,200 first-class games. He won 101 caps, a South American record, and took part in four World Cups, 1954, 1958, 1962 and 1966, gaining winners' medals in the 1958 and 1962 tournaments.

He and his full-back partner Nilton Santos, who was no relation, formed such

an authoritative understanding that they appeared in every match of the 1962 success.

Djalma was a popular choice for the Rest of the World team which played at Wembley in 1963 and he returned to England with Paolo Henrique as his partner for the 1966 World Cup finals, but by that time the Brazilians were in temporary decline and failed to qualify for the quarter-finals.

Those who followed Djalma's long and brilliant career will have their own particular memories of him. For me he must surely have reached the height of his skills in the 1962 World Cup finals. He looked a dominant figure when Brazil defeated England 3-1 at Vina Del Mar in a memorable quarter-final, an afternoon when the talent opposed to him included an attack of Bryan Douglas, Jimmy Greaves, Gerry Hitchens, Johnny Haynes and Bobby Charlton.

For almost an hour England matched the Brazilians but in the end it was the South Americans' better use of the ball, especially in build-up attacks, which won them the day. Needless to say, Djalma Santos was at the heart of their initial thrusts from the back.

Elisha Scott, who built a great reputation in goal for Liverpool, playing for Northern Ireland against England.

Elisha Scott

Northern Ireland, Liverpool, Belfast Celtic

Goalkeepers by the very nature of their role need to be consistently safe and courageous. It is the one position on the field where you can never 'hide' and leave the work to others. Throughout the long competitive history of the British game we have produced many 'keepers of special distinction. Such a one was Elisha Scott, a household name on Merseyside and in his native Ireland for 20 years or more.

Like so many of his breed Scott was a quiet, self-effacing person off the field. To meet him, without knowing of his capabilities as a goalkeeper, you might never guess that he could be transformed into a bundle of industry and agility once he pulled on his sweater. He had a fidgety style as he patrolled Liverpool's six-yard area, often jumping about even when play was nowhere near his goal. Yet this was not a nervous trait. By trial and error Scott had found that by

moving about all the time he kept his reflexes in sharp readiness for any attack launched upon him. His sense of anticipation was such that often he would pluck a ball out of the air when sections of the crowd were already hailing a goal. One of his greatest rivals was 'Dixie' Dean, the Everton centre-forward. Theirs was always a battle of wits. It was said on Merseyside that whenever the pair met in the street, 'Dixie' had only to nod his head in recognition for Scott to hurl himself across the pavement.

Liverpool were modest performers in the First Division when he signed for them from his home in Belfast in 1912. He soon gave authority to the last line of their defence and after finishing fourth in the first two post-war seasons, the 'Reds' won the Championship for the third time in their history (they had taken the title in 1901 and 1906). They won it most convincingly too, being six points clear of their nearest challengers, Tottenham Hotspur. The following season Liverpool retained the title and again it was by a clear margin of six points, from Sunderland.

By that time word of Scott's prowess had spread far and wide, and not least into the ears of the selectors in Belfast. They first chose him for the match with Scotland in Glasgow in March, 1920. The Irish lost 3-0 and Scott played seven internationals before he was to figure on a winning side. Appropriately, the occasion came in Belfast in February, 1926 when Wales were defeated 3-0. Altogether Scott was to represent his country 31 times, the last four after he had moved from Anfield in 1934 to take up an appointment as player-manager to Belfast Celtic. He was, in fact, aged 42 when he made his final appearance for Ireland in 1936. Once again Belfast was the venue and once more Wales were beaten to provide Scott with a fitting farewell to representative football.

During his long service to Liverpool FC he played in 429 League games.

152

Jimmy Seed

*England, Tottenham Hotspur,
Sheffield Wednesday*

Jimmy was a successful player who became a successful manager – and the two, as we all know, are by no means complementary. As inside-right for Spurs he laid on the pass from which Jimmy Dimmock shot the only goal of the game against Wolves in the 1921 FA Cup final at Stamford Bridge. Twenty-six years later he guided Charlton Athletic to victory over Burnley in the Final at Wembley, and once again it was a single goal which decided the outcome. One shudders to think how many cigars Jimmy must have smoked or chewed before Chris Duffy scored in the very last minute of extra time. Seed, of course, had taken Charlton to Wembley the previous year when the match also required an extra 30 minutes before Derby County triumphed 4-1.

Contemporaries of Seed tell me that he was an industrious inside-forward who shielded the ball cleverly and, like good wine, was at his best as he matured. Spurs discovered this to their cost when they decided to release him in 1927. He was then 32 but that did not deter Sheffield Wednesday from signing him and he repaid their faith by helping them to win the League Championship twice – in 1929 and 1930. To rub salt in the wound, Spurs were relegated in 1928.

While at White Hart Lane, Seed was capped five times for England – twice against the Belgians, one of the earliest opponents from abroad, and once each against Wales, Northern Ireland and Scotland.

He finished on the losing side only on his last appearance, a 2-0 defeat by Scotland in Glasgow in 1925.

When his playing days were over, Seed began a remarkable managerial partnership with Charlton, and in two years he took the club from the old Third Division South to runners-up position in the First Division. They won the Third Division title by a

Jimmy Seed (right) of champions Sheffield Wednesday shakes hands with opposing captain Wilson of Huddersfield before the 1930 FA Cup semi-final.

runaway eight points in season 1934-35, scoring 103 goals in 42 matches. The following season they finished one point behind the eventual Second Division champions, Manchester United, and while United went straight back down again, Charlton carried on their extraordinary run of successes by taking second place to Manchester City at the top of the First Division. This remains the highest position the club have attained since their election to the Football League in 1921. These were certainly palmy days at the Valley ground, and in February, 1938, there was a crowd of 75,031 who crammed in to watch an FA Cup fifth round tie with Aston Villa.

Immediately after the Second World War came Charlton's fine FA Cup performances but in September, 1956, Seed finally ended his association with the club which had lasted 23 years. Subsequently he took over the managership of Millwall and later served on their board of directors.

Uwe Seeler

West Germany, SV Hambourg

When Uwe Seeler retired in 1971 after 18 wonderful years in football the talk was about who would be his successor. It was stopped by Hambourg trainer Klaus Ochs, who said: 'There will be no new Uwe, now or ever. Uwe is the exception.'

That typified the special affection the Germans have for the man who captained them in two World Cups, 1966 and 1970, and shares with Pelé the distinction of having scored in four World Cup final tournaments.

When he finally said good-bye, with a host of world rivals involved in the first farewell match ever played in Germany, he had been capped by his country 72 times, more than any other player at that time.

Max Schmeling, the pre-war world heavyweight champion, can be the only other German sportsman whose popularity has approached Seeler's. For there has never been any breath of scandal about Seeler, who won the hearts of his countrymen when in April, 1961, he turned down a £60,000 offer from Inter Milan to stay with Hambourg.

The modest Seeler started as a striker and finished as a midfield general playing slightly more forward than usual. He was no flair player, just a fine honest professional whose experience was made to compensate for the absence of tricky stuff.

What country, club and fans got from Seeler was 120 per cent effort and enthusiasm. He was capable of scoring from almost any situation. He kept himself very fit, and many a defender, on the point of clearing, has been amazed to have the ball whipped away by a Seeler hurtling through the air with his head among the flying boots.

Of stocky build, he tended sometimes not to look quite the player he was. But there was little wrong with his ability to control

Uwe Seeler playing in his fourth World Cup finals in 1970. He scored in them all.

154

the ball and the last years of his period as a pure striker were played out with normally two defenders nipping at his heels.

His courage was never in question. His career was thought to have ended in 1956, when he was only 20, following a blow to his vertebrae. Eventually, after months of suffering pain after every match, he recovered. Two years later he was playing in the World Cup finals in Sweden.

Then, in 1963, he tore an achilles tendon. Once more his career was thought to be over. The tendon was shredded. But eight months after a four-hour operation Seeler was in the white of West Germany again.

He was top scorer in the Bundesliga five times. He led SV Hambourg to a European Cup Winners' Cup triumph in 1968. But the nicest gesture of them all was when they made him honorary captain of the West German national team.

Now that pleased a great patriot, and all his myriad friends in football.

Len Shackleton

England, Bradford Park Avenue,
Newcastle United, Sunderland

'The Clown Prince of Soccer.' That was Len Shackleton – a marvellous entertainer. Nobody who ever went to watch him was disappointed. Some time in every 90 minutes he would turn on something special.

He had his own way of playing the game. There was nothing a coach could do with him. Shack believed that in the 1940s and 1950s the game was still for enjoying, and enjoy it he did.

Many were the times he got so involved with the intricacies of what he was trying to do with the ball that he forgot the main purpose of the game. But the fans loved his brilliant ball play. They appreciated, too, the occasional Shackleton goal, scored just to show that scoring was not all that difficult.

As a poker player he would have been an artist, because he would throw the third

'Clown Prince of Soccer' Len Shackleton in Sunderland strip in 1956.

dummy when everybody had bought the first two. Nobody could believe the extent of his nerve.

In many ways, Shackleton could be categorised with Charlie Buchan, that Sunderland inside-forward of an earlier era. In many other ways, he was Buchan's opposite.

Apart from sharing the same position – and penchant for scoring goals from it – Buchan and Shackleton suffered similar experiences at Arsenal. Both were discarded at an early age, though while Buchan left after a dispute, Shackleton was simply told he was too frail.

He had been spotted by the Gunners while a schoolboy player in his native Bradford, and taken down to Highbury for trials.

Arsenal were in the midst of a spell where every other club in England looked up to them. It was every young man's dream to play for them. Probably Len Shackleton's dream, too. But Arsenal considered he did not match up to their standards, and they lived to regret it.

Disillusioned, but far from dispirited, Len went home to Yorkshire, signed for Bradford Park Avenue and then, with the war advancing, took a job down the pit.

His international bow, albeit an unofficial one, was in the Victory International against Scotland in April of 1946. It was a game that England have never cared to

Clever ball player Sivori played for Argentina and Italy as an inside-forward.

remember. Having dominated the wartime matches against Scotland, they lost this one 1-0.

A few months later, Shack was on his way from Bradford to Newcastle for what was then a sensational fee, £13,000. Any who doubted his worth were quashed convincingly when he scored six goals in his home debut against Newport.

To prove the point, Newcastle won promotion to the First Division in Len's first season at St James' Park. They also battled through to the semi-finals of the Cup, but an apparently rosy future was soured by internal unrest. Midway through the following season, Shackleton was allowed to cross the Tyne and Wear to neighbours Sunderland.

In the next ten years, he played more than 300 League games for Sunderland and was constantly regarded among the country's finest inside-forwards. But, maybe because he was thought to be too much an individualist, or maybe because his often wicked humour did not suit the selectors' taste, he won only five caps for England . . . another irony, as Buchan won exactly the same number.

His only goal for England was a superbly chipped effort in the 1954 game against West Germany – his last international. Sadly, for all his undoubted talent, he never won a club honour, either.

Shack's humour, perhaps tinged with a little bitterness, was reflected in his autobiography 'Clown Prince of Soccer'. One chapter was headed 'The average director's knowledge of football'. Under it, was a blank page.

Omar Sivori

Argentina, Italy, River Plate, Juventus, Napoli

Rated by John Charles as the best inside-forward he ever played with, Sivori was temperamental, but when in the mood, with all the off-field distractions behind

Joe Smith (with ball) leads out Bolton Wanderers for the 1926 FA Cup Final, the second of three Bolton victories in the 1920s.

him, a smooth and subtle performer.

He was a well-established international in his native Argentine in 1957 when Juventus chief Umberto Agnelli, then boss of the giant Fiat combine, began his campaign to make Juventus big enough to rival Real Madrid.

While he was negotiating with Leeds for Charles, he was also wheeling and dealing with River Plate to get Sivori. Charles came relatively cheap by Italian standards – he cost £57,000. But Argentinians drive a hard bargain and Agnelli was forced to raise the world transfer record to £91,000 to get little Sivori to Italy.

It was worth it. Juventus won the Italian League title three times in the next four seasons.

With Boniperti, later to become president of Juventus, Sivori and Charles formed a deadly trio. The tactic was comparatively simple. The other two would lie as far up-field as the Italian defensive system would allow and Sivori would push through a series of precisely weighted balls for them to run on to.

Sivori took a lot of punishment, but he could look after himself, too. The exchanges were certainly never allowed to become one-sided.

He had exceptional ball-control and a favourite trick of pushing the ball through opponents' legs. It did not endear him to the tough defenders of the time.

He could thump a ball, too. He scored 135 goals for Juventus before dropping down the soccer strata to Napoli in 1965.

Sivori's other claim to fame was that he once made a film with John Charles. Neither of them won an Oscar.

Joe Smith

England, Bolton Wanderers,
Stockport County

Joe Smith began his football career with Bolton Wanderers in 1908 and nearly 50 years later he managed Blackpool to an FA Cup final victory over his old club! The years between are littered with achievements. In season 1920-21, for instance, he headed the First Division list of scorers with 38 goals, which remains the highest tally obtained by a Bolton player. Two years later he captained Bolton to a 2-0 victory over West Ham

157

United in the first Wembley final, when an estimated quarter of a million arrived at the ground and thousands surged onto the pitch, and in 1926 he led the Wanderers to another Wembley triumph, this time by a 1-0 margin over Manchester City with the goal scored by David Jack. The Bolton forward line in those two finals makes impressive reading: Billy Butler, David Jack, J R Smith, Joe Smith and Ted Vizard.

Joe turned out in 450 League games for Bolton before joining Stockport County, but even that modest signing caused headlines. Apparently the transfer was completed without proper authority from the League and so Stockport were fined £125 and had two points deducted from their record.

In the summer of 1935 Blackpool appointed Joe manager and two years later he took the club up to the First Division, where under his guidance they came closest in their history to winning the Championship in season 1955-56. They finished second, though by the end the destination of the title was already long since decided with Manchester United 11 points ahead of the field!

Meanwhile Blackpool twice unsuccessfully appeared in FA Cup finals, first losing 4-2 to Manchester United in a match which some still regard as the finest played at Wembley, and then 2-0 to Newcastle United in 1951. But Joe's years of trying finally paid off with the memorable 1953 victory, in the game's final gasp, over Bolton Wanderers, the afternoon which earned Stanley Matthews that elusive Cup winners' medal when Blackpool won 4-3. Joe's feelings were slightly mixed that day.

Joe as a player was a foraging inside-forward with a powerful shot, and his partnership with Vizard was one of the best of its day. Despite his 450 League games for Bolton between 1908 and 1927 and all his obvious talents as a goalscoring inside-forward, he gained only five caps for England, three before the First World War and two immediately afterwards.

Luis Suarez

Spain, RCD, Barcelona, Inter-Milan, Sampdoria

Undoubtedly Luis Suarez is entitled to a place among the best of all the fine forwards produced by Spain. Yet for a player of such distinction at club level for Barcelona and in Italian football with Inter-Milan and Sampdoria of Genoa, he seldom rose to greatness at national and world competition.

Of course, he did have moments of splendour when wearing the international jersey, notably when Spain defeated the USSR 2-1 in Madrid in June, 1964, to carry off the European Nations' Cup in the second year of the tournament.

Overall, however, Suarez seemed a more potent force when playing regularly in a settled side, which he found both at Barcelona and during his Italian sojourn.

Suarez was born at Riazor, La Corunna and set out to become an electrician. He was still at the apprenticeship stage of the trade when, at the age of 18, he caused a big impression for his local club, RCD, against Barcelona. So much so, in fact, that Barcelona quickly offered RCD a fee of £14,000 for his transfer . . . and Suarez was launched on a footballing career that was constantly to find him in headline news.

In 1960 the football writers voted him European Footballer of the Year, after Barcelona had performed the domestic League and Cup double. And in 1961 Suarez's influence played an important part in his club reaching the final of the European Champions' Cup. However Barcelona were unable to continue the five successive victories of their Spanish rivals, Madrid, from 1956 to 1960, losing to Benfica by three goals to two in Berne.

A fresh and exciting challenge awaited Suarez that same year when Helenio Herrera, the most colourful and highly paid manager of his time, took him to Inter-Milan for a record fee at the time of

One of the best Spanish forwards of all time, Luis Suarez, who played in both Spain and Italy.

One of the best Spanish forwards of all time, Luis Suarez, who played in both Spain and Italy.

£210,000, of which the player is said to have received £59,000.

Herrera knew as much as anyone about Suarez, because before going to Italy, he had managed the Barcelona club, and his judgement was certainly not misplaced. With Suarez in the side Inter-Milan became Europe's most powerful club combination in the middle 1960s. They won the Italian Championship three times, in 1963, 1965 and 1966; the European Champions' Cup twice and the World Club Championship twice.

Suarez appeared in more than 200 League games for Inter before moving in 1970 to Sampdoria of Genoa, a young, promising team who clearly needed a 'general', a role which Suarez filled admirably.

What then were the qualities which made Suarez such a talked-about performer? Obviously he possessed physical power and a sharp awareness of situation, but to these attributes were added a shot of deadly effectiveness and ball control of adhesive characteristics. He could shift from one foot to the other or surge into top gear with the ball still answering implicitly to his commands.

He was still playing football as he approached his late thirties. By then the tempo of his game inevitably had altered but there was no disguising the artistry of the man.

Frank Swift

England, Manchester City

Not only was Frank Swift one of the best goalkeepers, he was also one of the most popular. Many a fan has gone home

This picture of Frank Swift shows his large hands wrapped round the ball. After his playing days, Swift was killed in the Munich air disaster.

treasuring a Big Swiftie wisecrack that has been thrown through the back of the net.

Frank's contribution to the game, of course, is far more important than that. He was probably the first of the great attacking goalkeepers.

Until the middle 1930s, the goalkeeper's role was purely defensive. He stopped the shots, ran towards the edge of his penalty area, booted the ball upfield and came back to watch the others get on with the business.

Swift realised this was a waste. He reasoned that while he had the ball his side were attacking. He found that he could throw the ball accurately some 30 and 40 yards, and so he perfected the tactic of clearing as often with a quick throw as he did with a slow kick.

Big Swiftie began life as a fisherman in Blackpool, and nets were to remain very much a part of his life until the Munich air disaster cut it short in his early forties.

His brother, Fred Swift, was another goalkeeper with Bolton, and in their 'teens they could often be found working together on their family's fishing boats. But at 17 years old, Frank was signed by Manchester City. He never played for another club.

Within two years of joining City, Swift was playing in an FA Cup final at Wembley. It began with a nightmare; Frank let a shot slip through his hands and City trailed Portsmouth 1-0 at half-time.

Two second-half goals from Freddy Tilson altered the balance, however. City won the Cup, but Frank, overcome by it all, passed out in his goalmouth at the sound of the final whistle.

He had to be assisted up to the Royal Box to collect his medal from King George V, who later sent a telegram to the club to enquire how the big man was. Frank treasured it until he died.

City won the League Championship three years later and Swift was inspiring. The very next year they were relegated to the Second Division, and Swift, by his own typically frank admission, could not have

stopped 'a fat pig in an alley'.

His slump in form was brief. The war found him playing for England, and when it was over, he helped City's immediate return to the First Division.

Swiftie played in 19 of England's first 20 internationals after the war. He also captained them twice, which says much for his colossal personality and leadership.

On and off the field, he was an entertainer –a vastly humorous man with a fund of stories and a sense of humour that continued even when the joke was on him.

In one match, a forward apparently threw mud into Frank's face. While he was blinded, the opposition scored. Frank's complaint to the referee that he could not see was greeted by 'Open your eyes then. And wash your face before you talk to me again.' Frank accepted it all.

Frank's image was as large as his physique. He was a joker, but talented enough for

people to laugh with him rather than at him.

He had enormous hands and a throw that would be the envy of any 'keeper. He could kick even farther and he was marvellously agile to go with it.

Perhaps his greatest performance was for England against Italy in Turin in 1948. Almost single-handed, he repelled one of Europe's finest attacks, while England scored four times for an illogically big win.

He made his last England appearance in the summer of 1949 and played his final game for City a few months later.

Nine years on, while working as a journalist covering the other Manchester club, United, he died.

Tostao

Brazil, Curziero, Vasco da Gama

One of the most under-rated of players, Tostao was a modern target man whose true

Tostao sidefoots the ball past the goalkeeper's dive for Brazil against Venezuela.

accomplishments were not appreciated until Brazil had to replace him for the 1974 World Cup.

Tostao's story is one of tragedy really, because an eye operation finished his career when he had so much more to offer.

How good was he, this elegant, white-faced Brazilian who roamed around opposing defences like a wraith? Anybody who can play in a World Cup final tournament between Pelé and Jairzinho and not be overshadowed has got to have something approaching greatness. And Tostao had.

He started with one big advantage. He was very intelligent. He graduated as an economist so perhaps solving problems in other people's penalty areas did not come too difficult. Tostao had the ability to make it look easy.

Tostao (left) shares the jubilation of Pelé (centre) and Jairzinho (right) after Pelé had opened the scoring against Italy in the 1970 World Cup Final.

from the tournament perhaps took some of the limelight off him, but back home he was helping Curziero win the Brazilian Cup in a competition usually won by clubs from the big city areas of Rio and Sao Paulo.

All seemed well with Tostao's world when Brazil had taken their place among the appointed qualifiers for Mexico. Until a football hit him on the back of his head. It was a freak accident because it detached a retina.

He was flown to Houston for surgery, and was right for the World Cup finals and the winner's medal he deserved so much.

Eventually, Tostao succumbed to the lure of the big-time. Rio's Vasco da Gama offered Curziero £220,000 for the World Cup star. He went, but that eye was never as good as it was before the accident.

Tostao was expected to be one of the dominant figures when the World Cup finals were played in West Germany in 1974, but he missed out.

Too wise to take a chance with eyesight, he became a very successful businessman owning, among other companies, a chain of garages. Tostao was used to being in the driving seat.

Ivo Viktor

Czechoslovakia, Dukla Prague

Before the war it used to be said that the continent of Europe could not produce good goalkeepers. They were all arm wavers who played to the gallery.

Well, all that has changed now and one of the men who have changed it is Ivo Viktor, who first played for Czechoslovakia back in 1965 and from then on was a fixture in the national team for years.

Dependability is the name of the Viktor game and it is no coincidence that usually Czechoslovakia have achieved good results in his time.

In the early 1970s they were one of the strongest teams in Europe, good enough to knock England out of the Nations Cup

He had the nous to know where to go and when to go. Very rarely did Tostao seem to run. He glided, with a gift akin to Muller's of arriving on the ball when least expected.

A drop of the shoulders, a flick of the head, a slight turn of the foot, and Tostao had done the damage before the bemused defence realised that there was any danger.

He was at his best in the qualifying rounds for the 1970 World Cup. The rest of the world had trouble spelled out to them by his nine goals on the way to Mexico. It nailed the belief that he was not much of a shot.

European experts should have done their homework better. He was only 19 when he came to England as a member of Brazil's 1966 World Cup party, and he scored against Hungary. Brazil's early dismissal tournament without too much trouble.

As Viktor's number of caps neared the 100 mark he was able to look back on an international career in which he conceded an average of not much more than a goal a match.

He takes after English goalkeepers in that he has good anticipation, and does not fall for the Continental fault of straying too far out of goal, at least not since Pelé almost beat him with that 50-yard lob in the 1970 World Cup.

Viktor spent his youth in the Army and was flattered to find when he came out that ten clubs were angling for his services.

Right **Ivo Viktor, one of the best of the world's modern goalkeepers.**

Below **Ivo Viktor punches the ball from the head of England's Martin Dobson during a European Championship match in 1974. Czechoslovakia went on to win the trophy.**

He is honest about why he chose Dukla and went straight into their reserve team. 'I could have gone into the senior teams of those other clubs, but they might have struggled and lost their place in the senior division.

'The only way I was going to achieve my ambition to play for my country was to be with the top club. So I had to become Dukla's No. 1 goalkeeper first, and within a season and a half of joining them I was.'

That is the sort of singlemindedness that has kept Viktor at the top so long.

Valeri Voronin

Russia, Moscow Torpedo

It is argued many times that the Russians make dull footballers. It is a myth. From Yashin downwards they have given the game some fine goalkeepers. They have usually had a striker who has become something of a personality, too.

And they have always had an eye-catching midfield man. Voronin, the man who took over from Netto, was such a player.

In Voronin's peak in the early and mid-1960s, Russia became one of the first countries to try the 4-4-2 system which Brazil used in the 1962 World Cup.

For them, it was something of a success – because Voronin adapted from traditional right-half to become the presiding genius.

Like most exceptional players, he was attack-minded, especially happy when going forward with unusual grace.

Torpedo were quick to spot the unusual talent. He was only 18, young by Russian standards, when he forced his way into the first team, and once there he was rarely out of it. He was something of a Johnny Haynes player in that he could see the killer pass slightly earlier than most, and although he lacked the pin-point accuracy of Haynes, he compensated by using surprise.

By 1962 he had become Russia's most important player in the Chile World Cup finals, despite having won his first cap

Valeri Voronin, a Russian footballer of considerable flair.

barely twelve months earlier.

Russia's Footballer of the Year in 1964, older Spanish fans still talk about his fine display in the 1964 European Nations Cup Final when Russia lost to Spain.

Billy Walker

England, Aston Villa

Two clubs, Aston Villa and Nottingham Forest, received wonderful service from Billy Walker, stretching over more than 40 years, and his name is remembered with affection by countless numbers of supporters at Villa Park and the City ground.

Billy who was born at Wednesday in Staffordshire, first came into prominence in his early twenties when he was called up for the first time by Villa for an FA Cup-tie in January, 1920. He had joined the club the previous year and he remained with them until 1934. During that period he made almost 500 League appearances and scored 213 goals, which is still a club record shared with Harry Hampton.

Billy originally made his mark as a centre-forward but his true talents were best expressed when he moved to inside-left. In his new position he took on the role of scheming Villa's raids, using close dribbling skills allied to body swerves to confuse opponents. They seldom knew whether he was simply setting up scoring situations for those around him or planning a shot. He moved so swiftly that many of his goals were struck after defenders had been deceived into moving off him to cover the anticipated pass.

Villa were in dire straits at the foot of the First Division in season 1919-20, but the transfer of Frank Barson, a hard-tackling centre-half from Barnsley, brought a transformation in the club's fortunes. The tenaciousness of Barson in midfield and Walker's gifts as a striker provided the springboard for Villa's resurgence.

They reached the FA Cup final that season and, under Walker's captaincy, they beat Huddersfield Town 1-0 after extra time at Stamford Bridge. That was the club's sixth success although they had to wait a further 37 years before establishing a record of seven FA Cup final victories. Billy was at inside-left for Villa's next Cup final appearance in 1924 when Wembley was the venue. But this time Newcastle won 2-0.

The England selectors began to take notice of him and he was given the first of his 18 caps against Northern Ireland at Sunderland in October, 1920, when he led the attack and scored a goal in a 2-0 win. Twice he scored two goals in matches against foreign opposition, first against Sweden in Stockholm and then against Belgium at West Bromwich.

Management seemed to follow naturally for Billy once he decided to quit as a player. He accepted the job at Hillsborough in November, 1933, and two years later plotted Sheffield Wednesday's path to FA Cup

Captain of Aston Villa, Billy Walker was a prolific goal-scoring inside-forward.

glory at Wembley where West Bromwich Albion were beaten 4-2. Subsequently he spent a period with a non-League club, Chelmsford, before starting his long association with Nottingham Forest in 1939.

In 1959 he went back to Wembley after much nail-biting en route. In the third round Forest almost went out to a non-League side, Tooting, on a snow-covered pitch. They were held to a 2-2 draw after being two behind, but won the replay 3-0. After comfortably disposing of Grimsby, they shared two 1-1 draws with Birmingham City before triumphing 5-0 in the third game. Victories by 2-1 and 1-0 over Bolton and Aston Villa (his old club) took Walker and his side into the final.

Roy Dwight opened the scoring for Forest but later was carried off with a broken leg, an incident which cast something of a cloud over his team's 2-1 victory over Luton Town. Billy retired as manager in 1960.

Looking back over his long life in the game, I discovered one other unusual record which goes down to his name. In November, 1921, he scored three goals from penalties against Bradford City – and I can well imagine the cunning with which he deceived the 'keeper that afternoon!

Fritz Walter

West Germany, Kaiserlautern

World Cup-winning captains are somewhat hard to come by. In fact, until the next finals in Spain in 1982 there have been only 11 of them, and to be honest Fritz Walter was one of the most unlikely.

Not because he was less than an exceptional player – he was all of that – but because he carried off the trophy in Switzerland in 1954 when the entire tournament had seemed not much more than a formality

World Cup-winning captain in 1954, Fritz Walter also had his brother in the West German side.

for the great Hungarians.

It is one of soccer's great sagas now, the story of how Germany beat the favourites 3-2 in a Final which Walter, a masterly inside-forward, did more than any other German player to win.

Walter played 61 games for West Germany but never one as tremendous as that. After only eight minutes, Germany were two goals down and the Final seemed to be over. But Walter made the first goal for Morlock and the winner for Rahn.

At 29, Walter, after that great triumph, could have been considered to have had his day. That was not Walter's way of seeing it, and he was in Sweden for the World Cup finals four years later when he led the Cup-holders as far as the semi-finals.

No brilliant individualist, Walter's greatest virtue was his ability to read a game. He was the ideal middle of the field man, able to control balls played out of defence quickly and distribute them shrewdly.

There was more of the typical German in Walter than, say, Beckenbauer. He played within his limitations. He delivered the 60-40 ball, not the one with only a 50-50 chance.

A wartime paratrooper, he scored 33 international goals.

Ray Wilson

England, Huddersfield Town, Everton, Oldham Athletic, Bradford City

Ray Wilson, quiet, unassuming, modest to the point of virtually opting out of the game when he finished playing, could easily be rated one of the most effective full-backs England have been lucky enough to produce.

Not a tall fellow, but very nimble, he had the pace and the agility to get back with fast-moving forwards when they broke away from him.

Wilson's great forte was not that he did anything brilliantly. He did not. He just never did anything wrongly. That fact alone spells out the sort of player he was.

166

A solid defensive player, Ray Wilson gets up to clear the England lines.

Like every member of England's 1966 World Cup-winning side he had to be able to do a bit with the ball. He could. Like Bobby Moore alongside him, he just hated wasting it.

When England won the World Cup in 1966, it was the names of Hurst, Banks, Moore and Bobby Charlton which stole the headlines; the personalities of Jack Charlton and Stiles which captured the public's imagination.

Few people spent much time on the name, the style or the image of Ray Wilson, although most experts agreed that his play at left-back was one of the major contributory factors in England's triumph.

Wilson was a quiet man and a quietly effective player. Unlike George Cohen, his full-back partner for 28 of his 63 inter-

nationals, he was not renowned for the spectacular overlap. He was, nevertheless, one of the most solid defensive players England has ever boasted in that position – and he added the quality of accurate distribution.

Born at Shirebrook in Derbyshire in 1935, Ray made his League debut for Huddersfield 20 years later and stayed there for nine seasons, despite numerous offers from First Division clubs.

In his time there, Huddersfield never climbed out of the Second Division, but Wilson was consistently impressive enough to become a regular player in Walter Winterbottom's England team.

Bill Shankly was, for some time, Wilson's manager at Huddersfield, and spent much of his time repelling offers for his prize full-back. So it was something of an irony that, in 1964, five years after Shanks had departed to become a legend at Anfield, Wilson was

finally sold for £40,000 . . . to Liverpool's next-door neighbours Everton.

Everton were League Champions when Wilson joined. In his second season at Goodison, they won the FA Cup, beating Sheffield Wednesday 3-2. Two years later they were back at Wembley, losing this time, by the only goal at West Bromwich Albion.

There was never any dispute, however, that Ray's great days came in July of 1966, when he was ever-present in England's march to become World Champions.

By 1969, his playing career was into its dying stages. Everton gave him a free transfer after a lengthy lay-off with knee trouble. He was signed by Oldham, but played only 25 times for them before moving again, on another free transfer, to Bradford City.

He played the last two League games of his career for City. The 1970-71 season was his last, and although he flirted briefly with a managerial job at the club, he could not relate to the different demands and decided to take a job completely unconnected with football.

Ray Wilson, World Cup winner of 1966, joined the family business, and when last I heard he was doing very nicely, thank you . . . as a funeral director in Huddersfield, the town where it all began.

Billy Wright

England, Wolves

Billy Wright was another of those players who defied the law of gravity, or seemed to. For a man of his short height he hung in the air a long time to win the ball.

It was that ability that enabled him to move from right-half to centre-half and so extend his record-breaking run in England's team for several seasons.

He graduated from being a strong-tack-

Ray Wilson was stylish enough to command a regular England place while playing with Huddersfield Town in the Second Division.

168

ling, good-passing wing-half into a most stubborn centre defender. He was the first Englishman to pass a century of caps, a tribute to his stamina and his knack of producing innumerable performances with very few blemishes.

Consistency was the cornerstone of his career. He was quick into the tackle and quick to use the ball when he had it. He could go round a player or two if he had to, but he would much rather the ball did the work.

He had total dedication to the game. He was a fitness fanatic and wonderful enthusiasm made him an inspirational captain. He was prepared to cover every blade of grass on the pitch, and never expected any of his colleagues to do a job he would not do himself.

The fairy-tale began early for Billy Wright. His Football League debut for Wolves was at the opening of the 1946-47 season. Within less than two months, he was in the England team which thrashed Ireland 7-2 in Belfast.

Thirteen years later, he was to play his 105th, and last, international. Wright was 35 then, and England beat the United States 8-1 in Los Angeles.

Sandwiched between these dates was a story that most modern script-writers would reject as absurdly fanciful.

Yet Wright was not a spectacular player or a spectacular person. At left-half, and latterly at centre-half, he was assured and reliable. Off the field, he was modest, unaffected.

By the age of 24 he was captaining club and country. He led England for the first time in 1948, against Ireland in Belfast, and a year later he was marching up the steps to Wembley's Royal Box to collect the FA Cup for Wolves.

It was all quite an irony, really. When he was 15, Wright was firmly advised to go

Billy Wright was the first Englishman to win 100 caps, many of them as captain.

home by the then Wolves manager, Major Frank Buckley, who thought him too small and simply not up to standard. Buckley was later to be very thankful that he had changed his mind.

Wolves had never won the League Championship until Wright led them to it in 1954. Four years later, he did it again, retaining the title for a second season in 1959, the final season of his momentous career.

The club matches that stir Billy's memory, however, are those significant floodlit affairs during 1954, when Wolves defeated Spartak of Moscow and Honved of Budapest in fixtures that acted as catalysts in the construction of the European club competitions we now know so well.

Despite his 490 League appearances and countless honours gained at Wolves, however, Billy will be remembered – by me and by almost every other English football lover – as the man who created a new record of 105 international caps.

Not surprisingly, he treasures the 100th more than any other, and for more than the obvious reasons. On the day that his selection was announced, his wife Joy – one of the singing Beverley Sisters – gave birth to their first child. Match day saw all three of the sisters in the stand at Wembley, dressed in England white.

England lost 21 times in Wright's 105 matches, 90 of which he played as captain. But it was typical of the man that he opted to leave the game, not in a blaze of trumpets, but in the calm of a pre-season friendly in the autumn of 1959. Significantly, however, 20,000 people turned up to pay their own tribute.

Lev Yashin

Russia, Moscow Dynamo

There can be no prizes for naming the most popular Russian footballer of them all. Lev Yashin is the answer. Making his club debut in 1951, he was European Footballer of the Year in 1963. That year he was the only possible choice to keep goal for the Rest of the World when they met England at Wembley. He was the USSR's World Cup goalkeeper in 1966 when within punching distance of his 40th birthday.

Left **Billy Wright shakes hands with the linesman before the England-Italy match, Wembley, 1959.**

Below **Lev Yashin grabs the ball to foil England's marksman Jimmy Greaves.**

The most popular Russian footballer, Lev Yashin, dives at Uwe Seeler's feet in the World Cup semi-finals of 1966.

Yet as a schoolboy, Yashin was a complete sporting failure. He was also thought of as something of a freak, and the jibes he took for his unusual height provoked him into countless playground scraps. Most of them, he lost convincingly.

He was born in 1929, first went to school at seven years old and was working in an aircraft factory by the time he was 14.

Under the strong influence of his father, who desperately wanted a sporting son, Lev tried athletics, boxing, basketball, ice hockey . . . he tried the lot, and failed.

Finally, he broke through, winning a

place in the factory football team—as a forward. He still says that his ambition had always been to play at the front and score goals. Goalkeeper was a position that never entered his plans.

Lev finally had to face facts, however. He was no forward, even at factory level. Gradually, he was 'relegated' through the ranks until one match found him as the goalkeeper. He stayed there for the rest of his career.

Yashin was called up for army service in 1949 and found himself with another sporting talent. He soon won a place in the hockey section of the club he was to serve for the rest of his life—the famous KGB club, Dynamo.

It naturally followed that Lev should

was also given two high Russian honours – the Order of Lenin and the Honoured Master of Sport. Yet, he remained a modest individual, both in temperament and life-style, living in a two-roomed flat in Moscow.

Out of football, Yashin became a sergeant in the Soviet internal security police. On the field, he became known as 'Panther', and made the all-black strip his trademark.

Yashin spent several years of his playing life 'on the road' with the Russian side, who made it their policy to tour the world, keeping a squad together for major tournaments. Training demands were harsh and the great goalkeeper relates that he eventually tired of incessant travelling.

He appeared in three World Cups, his brilliance helping Russia into fourth place in England in 1966. With Dynamo, he won five Championship medals and two Cup-winners' medals.

When he retired in 1970, Dynamo met the Rest of the World in a grand testimonial that drew 100,000 people to the Lenin Stadium. Russian football may never see his like again.

George Young

Scotland, Glasgow Rangers

become interested in the Dynamo football team, and, indeed, he developed something of a hero-worship for their goalkeeper, Alexei Khomich.

Two years later, in 1951, Yashin was on the Dynamo bench when Khomich was injured. Lev replaced his idol and made his debut – disastrously. Within minutes of stepping on the pitch, Yashin had conceded a goal.

It takes more than one error to write off a 'keeper, however, and Yashin quickly demonstrated that he had a special talent. Five years later, he was to win his first international honour, keeping goal for the Russian national side which took the Olympic gold medal in Melbourne.

Lev went on to win 78 caps for Russia. He

Between 1946-47 and 1956-57 when he sensibly decided to get out while he was at the top, George Young, man-mountain right-back or centre-half of Rangers, was Scottish football.

In 11 seasons he played 53 times for Scotland, most of them as captain. Who else would they have nominated? Scotland have often been pilloried for coming later than most to the business of appointing a team-manager. With Big George in the side they hardly needed one.

George had no aspirations to become a ball player. At 6ft 2in and over 15st that would have been more than a shade optimistic. He could hardly develop into a greyhound either.

But as a reader of the game from the back,

George Young (left) looks on as a shot from England goes over the Scottish bar at Hampden Park, 1956.

they did not come any better. When he was criticised as a defender who could do nothing but bang the ball up the field, his reply was that it was deliberate. Rangers and Scotland were playing the long-ball game under George Young just as Wolves, south of the border, were doing under Billy Wright.

Willie Waddell played long enough on Scotland and Rangers' right wing to know what Young could do and he always swears he was a better passer of a ball than most. The truth is that the only people who would disagree that Young was clumsy would be opposition forwards.

Young had no nerves. He scored two penalties, cool as you like, against Clyde in 1949 Cup final. Four years later, he brought the house down by playing in goal and earning a cup replay against an astounded Aberdeen side.

Young was a very fit 35 when he was

suddenly dropped from the Scotland side without any explanation. Perhaps the powers that be at that time thought Young was exerting too much influence around the circuit.

The decision hurt Young, who reckoned he was capable of going on for another couple of seasons, and he retired.

He managed Third Lanark for a time but then took over a hotel. That decision by the Scotland selectors left a scar that never quite healed. I feel sure that Scotland lost more than Young did.

Dino Zoff

Italy, Udinese, Mantova, Naples, Juventus

It is impossible, in a book of this description, to prevent the last place going to Dino Zoff, who almost certainly set up a soccer record that will never be broken.

He kept goal in more than ten consecutive Italy matches – 1,143 minutes to be precise – without conceding a goal. The run came to an end while Italy were playing Haiti in the

1974 World Cup. Zoff did not play for Italy in the 1970 and 1966 World Cups and only the selectors can know why Albertosi was preferred. He was, however, the captain of Italy in the 1978 World Cup.

It could be that the amiable Zoff, a perfectionist in practice, has got better as he has grown older. His study of the principles of acrobatics has paid off, but that knowledge would have been of little use without skill and bravery, qualities on which Zoff is not short.

It took Zoff a long time to live among the famous. He made his Italian League debut in 1961, spent six years getting to Naples, but then in 1972 commanded a big fee to sign for Juventus.

He was voted No. 2 in the European Footballer of the Year poll in 1973, confirming that recognition was a long time coming. He had been in goal when Italy won the European Championship in 1968, but it is the magic 1,143 minutes of soccer leading up to Sanon's goal for Haiti in 1974 by which Zoff will be always remembered.

Above **Zoff, who captained Italy in the 1978 World Cup finals, clears from Pearson, of England.**

Below **Dino Zoff, unbeaten in internationals for Italy for 1,143 minutes before Haiti scored in the World Cup of 1974.**

Photographic acknowledgements

Black and white
Bavaria–Verlag, Munich 1; Central Press Photos Ltd., London 152, 164; Colorsport, London front and back endpapers, 8, 9, 10, 13, 15, 20, 21, 24–25, 28, 29, 34, 38 top, 41, 42, 44, 45, 49, 51 bottom, 52, 53, 55, 57, 59, 65, 68, 72, 75 top, 84, 85, 88–89, 90, 91, 93, 96, 108, 112, 116, 119, 122, 128, 133, 137, 139, 144, 145, 148, 149, 155, 165, 168, 169, 175 bottom; Fox Photos Ltd., London 127; Hungarian Embassy, London 32–33, 97, 146–147; Keystone Press Agency, London 39, 126; Novosti Press Agency, London 141 left; Popperfoto, London 30, 80–81, 118; Press Association, London 17 top, 60–61, 63, 75 bottom, 76, 77, 106, 110, 111, 129, 159 top, 163 bottom, 172–173, 174; Radio Times Hulton Picture Library, London 16–17, 37, 101, 104–105, 114 bottom, 121, 131, 153; Sport & General Press Agency, London 31, 141 right, 146 bottom, 151, 166; Syndication International Ltd., London 60 top, 69, 102, 123, 125, 157, 159 bottom, 160–161, 162; Ullstein Bilderdienst, Berlin–Schirner 156.

Colour
All-sport Photographic Ltd., Morden 2–3, 6, 11, 14, 19, 38 bottom, 54, 58, 70, 86–87, 103, 138; BBC Copyright Photograph, London 7; Colorsport, London 22, 26, 35, 46, 50–51, 66, 74, 83, 94, 98, 99, 114 top, 115, 134–135, 143, 150, 163 top, 175 top; Ray Green, Cheadle 67; Press Association, London 27, 43, 62, 82, 167, 171; Sporting Pictures (UK) Ltd., London 107, 154; Syndication International Ltd., London 170.